TRANSFORMATIONS OF GENDER IN MELANESIA

TRANSFORMATIONS OF GENDER IN MELANESIA

EDITED BY MARTHA MACINTYRE AND CERIDWEN SPARK

Australian
National
University

PRESS

PACIFIC SERIES

ANU PRESS

Published by ANU Press
The Australian National University
Acton ACT 2601, Australia
Email: anupress@anu.edu.au
This title is also available online at press.anu.edu.au

National Library of Australia Cataloguing-in-Publication entry

Title: Transformations of gender in Melanesia / Martha Macintyre,
                        Ceridwen Spark, editors.

ISBN: 9781760460884 (paperback) 9781760460891 (ebook)

Subjects: Women--Melanesia--Social conditions.
                        Women--Melanesia--Economic conditions.
                        Women's rights--Melanesia
                        Social change--Melanesia.
                        Culture and globalization--Melanesia.

Other Creators/Contributors:
                        Macintyre, Martha, editor.
                        Spark, Ceridwen, 1971- editor.

Cover design and layout by ANU Press. Cover photograph by Ceridwen Spark.

The book is dedicated to the memory of Naomi Yupae (1957–2016), the inaugural executive director and one of the founders of Eastern Highlands Family Voice (EHFV), an organisation that supports families experiencing violence and conflict in Papua New Guinea.

Contents

Acknowledgements

Most of these essays began as presentations in a panel we co-chaired at the State of the Pacific conference at The Australian National University in 2014. The 'panel on gender' frequently represents the only time when masculinity and femininity are discussed as though they have a bearing on the 'real' issues in the Pacific—security, economic development and politics. But this time was different—the conference began for instance with an inspiring keynote address by Amanda Donigi, a young Papua New Guinean entrepreneur who founded and runs *Stella* magazine. For organising the conference in such a way that gender and Pacific women were front and centre, we thank Tim Sharp and John Cox.

For their commitment to redrafting chapters, we would like to thank our contributing authors who have been patient and responsive. Comments from reviewers were insightful and in the best sense demanding, and we thank the reviewers for assisting us to improve our original drafts to make this a stronger collection. Thanks also to Carolyn Brewer for her editing work and to the publications team at ANU Press. Ceridwen is also grateful to the School of Global, Urban and Social Studies at RMIT University for the grant that supported the costs of publication.

Finally, for permission to use the photo on the cover we thank the subjects, Rachael Billy Ipai and Charlie Andrew, employees of Pacific Towing (PNG) Ltd, and Neil Papenfus, the General Manager of Pacific Towing, for helping to facilitate this permission.

Abbreviations

AusAID	Australian Agency for International Development
CEDAW	Convention on the Elimination of All Forms of Discrimination against Women
CFC	Christian Fellowship Church
CPCHE	Canadian Partnership for Children's Health and Environment
DAWN	Development Alternatives with Women for a New Era
DFAT	Department of Foreign Affairs and Trade
FPTP	first-past-the-post
FSII	Forum Solomon Islands International
FSM	Federated States of Micronesia
FSVU	Family and Sexual Violence Unit
FWRM	Fiji Women's Rights Movement
ICTs	information communication technologies
IPPF	International Planned Parenthood Federation
IPO	Interim Protection Order
IWDA	International Women's Development Agency
LTEU	Letters to the Editor Uncensored
MEHRD	Ministry of Education and Human Resources Development, Solomon Islands
MP	Member of Parliament

MSF	Médecins Sans Frontières (Doctors Without Borders)
NGO	non-government organisation
PACWIP	Pacific Women in Politics
PNG	Papua New Guinea
PYWLA	Pacific Young Women's Leadership Alliance
RCDF	Rural Constituency Development Fund
RPNGC	Royal Papua New Guinea Constabulary
SIA	Security Industries Association/Authority
SPC	Secretariat of the Pacific Community
SSEC	South Seas Evangelical Church
UNFPA	United Nations Population Fund
UNICEF	United Nations Children's Fund
UNIFEM	United Nations Development Fund for Women
WISDM	Women In Shared Decision-Making
YWCA	Young Women's Christian Association

Introduction: Flux and change in Melanesian gender relations

Martha Macintyre

University of Melbourne

The chapters in this volume began as papers at the State of the Pacific conference at The Australian National University in 2014. My own contribution there was a simple reflection on the ideas of change and transition in gender relations in Papua New Guinea, the country in which I have conducted most of my research. In introducing the chapters I have retained many of my initial observations about transformations of gender relations in Papua New Guinea, but have attempted to draw comparisons in order to illustrate broad themes that have been the subjects of inquiry and the markers of changing gender distinctions in Melanesia. The concepts of change, transformation and transition are imbued with ideas of development and progress—notions themselves that have been subject to criticism for being redolent of colonial ideologies. Whether we consider Melanesian modernity and the move of Melanesia into a globalised world to be 'progress' or a further instance of neo-colonialism, many people in this region now live in towns and work in paid employment or worry about their inability to do so. They communicate using mobile phones and the internet; they debate women's rights and roles in society, drawing upon discourses of human rights and the goals of United Nations agencies. The chapters in this volume document and analyse some of the ways that Melanesians negotiate and embrace changes in their lives, their personal and political aspirations and the tensions between conceptions of gender relations in the past, difficulties in the present and aspirations for the future.

Gender, independence and women leaders

The various architects of independent self-government for Pacific nations were generally optimistic liberals on the subject of gender. In each of the countries discussed in this volume, women and men were guaranteed equal rights as citizens in their new constitutions. Unlike European, American and Australian women, Pacific women did not have to struggle to be enfranchised. They were not legally excluded from educational or employment opportunities, nor were there constraints on their rights to hold property. Similarly, men in Pacific countries were granted suffrage without the contestations over class, land ownership, property and other factors that had been central to the campaigns for manhood suffrage in other countries. Yet the assumptions about equality that were held by those who wrote gender equity into their constitutions were rapidly proven false or inadequate in the years following independence. While men eagerly sought tertiary education, embraced new roles in politics and public administration and started commercial enterprises, relatively few Pacific women did so.

This should not have been surprising. After all, in all Pacific countries prior to independence, most of the political, administrative and business roles had been occupied by (white) men, and Pauline Soaki notes in her chapter the historical determinants of contemporary structural inequity. Education for girls, especially at secondary and tertiary levels, had been limited in the years leading up to independence. The business of governing, legislating and providing services was already established as primarily a male preserve. In short, the ideals of gender equality enshrined in constitutions were going to be difficult to achieve given the legacies of colonialism and the structural barriers that women faced.

Nonetheless, in each country, there were some women who were able to take advantage of the aspirations of new nationhood. I recall my first trip to Papua New Guinea in 1979 when I visited several government departments and encountered a number of Papua New Guinean women who held senior positions in the administration. In thinking about the recent changes in gender relations discussed in this volume, where women appear to be gaining ground, the extraordinary women who preceded them need to be acknowledged. In the 1980s, only 18 per cent of public servants were women and the majority were in low-level clerical jobs. But there were women who held very senior government positions. To mention just a few: Margaret Nakikus was the Director of the National

Planning Office; Felecia Dobunaba became Secretary of the Department of Welfare; Rose Kekedo headed the Department of Community and Family Services; Naomi Martin, the first PNG woman to obtain a PhD, became the head of the Commission for Higher Education; Meg Taylor was an advisor to the first Prime Minister, Michael Somare, later becoming Ambassador to the United States, Mexico and Canada. The list could be extended. These women were trailblazers who faced forms of gender discrimination but were able to succeed in high-profile careers.

In all of the countries that feature in this collection women faced similar barriers. In Solomon Islands, Lily Ogatina Poznanski was the first woman elected to political office in 1965—a considerable achievement prior to independence when women were unable to vote. Since then women have contested seats in every election, although the number who have won seats remains low. But, as in Papua New Guinea, during the 1970s and 1980s a number of highly educated women gained senior positions in the public service. Phyllis Taloikwai was the first woman to become a permanent secretary; Joy Kere was appointed Chief Planning Officer in the Health Planning Unit; and others followed in their wake in the decades that followed. In Vanuatu only four women have been elected to parliament since 1980 and there are currently no female members of parliament, but women such as Hilda Lini and Grace Molisa held senior posts in government administrations during the colonial period and were prominent in debates about the role of women in the postcolonial state. In 1966, in Fiji, Adi Losalini Dovi was the first woman to become a member of parliament. Nominated by the Council of Chiefs, her election owed much to her status in the hierarchy, but she did continue as an elected member for more than a decade. Fiji currently has a higher percentage of women in parliament (16 per cent) than any other Pacific nation.

Despite being the most populous and richest country in Melanesia, Papua New Guinea's record on gender equity is poor. Since 1964, when all adult men and women gained the vote, only six women have been elected to parliament. For many years, Dame Carol Kidu was the sole voice for women. Only three women have ever been elected as heads of provincial government: in Morobe, Enny Moaitz; in Milne Bay, Dame Josephine Abaijah; and Julie Soso in Eastern Highlands Province. While the number of women in politics and senior administrative positions is a relatively simple way of assessing gender equity in those spheres, achieving an increase in female participation has been a goal set by external agencies such as the United Nations and Australian Agency for International

Development (AusAID) (now DFAT (the Department of Foreign Affairs and Trade)). As the chapters in this volume attest, women's political leadership is not the primary objective of many Pacific women who are deeply committed to changing the lives and status of women in their countries.

In Papua New Guinea, Vanuatu and Solomon Islands, most of the women who held high office in the early years of independence had been educated first at mission schools, with a few attending schools in Australia and New Zealand. Several went on to universities in England, Australia and the United States, as well as the newly established University of Papua New Guinea and University of the South Pacific. Rose Kekedo, who held managerial positions in government, educational administration and commerce, commented in an interview: 'There are many high hurdles to vault and many barriers to overcome. A woman pursuing a career must be strong to withstand the pressures of working in "a man's world"' (cited in Turner 1993: 98). But during this period there were numerous women who were outstanding leaders in fields dominated by men, not only in Papua New Guinea, but also in Fiji, where Adi Losalini Dovi and Irene Jai Narayan both attained high political office. In Vanuatu, Grace Mera Molisa became second secretary of the Ministry of Social Affairs in 1979, and Hilda Lini was the first woman elected to parliament.

The first wave of women holding political office and occupying senior public service positions provided the next generation with role models and showed that women were capable of leadership that commanded the respect of men and women who worked with them. But since independence the percentage of women in Pacific national parliaments has never risen above 10 per cent, and in 2015 it stood at 6 per cent. In Fiji, Solomon Islands and Vanuatu, similar trends to those outlined for Papua New Guinea can be observed. Pauline Soaki's chapter documents some of the problems that women political candidates face in Solomon Islands—problems also encountered by women in all other Pacific countries (PACWIP n.d.).

Development aspirations

Notions of capitalist economic progress and the consolidation of political systems, which draw on Western liberal ideals of democratic representation and the individual liberty of all citizens, inspire international programs aiming to improve the status of women in developing countries. Liberal feminist objectives in the West emphasised gender equity and equality, politically and economically, in ways consonant with their economic and political systems. While some of these ideals find a 'fit' with people and governments in emergent Pacific nations, others seem alien or inappropriate. Understandings of gender relations and social distinction that people locate in a precolonial past (as custom or tradition) are perceived by some as incompatible with introduced ideas of citizenship and equality. However, the complex entanglement of social relations based in precolonial systems with those of colonialism, Western education, new economic forms and Christian adherence belies this simplistic division into intrinsic and introduced.

Pacific women measure the advancement of their interests in many fields apart from political leadership. The processes of transformation in gender categories and gender relations discussed in this collection have a history. From the first waves of European colonisation and missionary activity in the Pacific (Choi and Jolly (eds) 2014; Jolly and Macintyre 1989), existing social and cultural norms have been challenged and changed by exogenous agents. Sometimes the changes have been embraced, sometimes rejected or resisted. The establishment of mission schools for girls across the region and the development of organisations such as the Young Women's Christian Association (YWCA) and the Girl Guides, as well as church-based women's organisations, set in train new ways for women to define and pursue their collective interests. Parochial institutions, that might at first seem to have been imposed by outsiders bent on recasting the lives of women and girls, rapidly became 'vernacularised' and provided some of the means of managing their changed circumstances (Douglas 2003; McDougall 2003; Pollard and Waring (eds) 2010).

Interpreting gender: Anthropology and development studies

Since the late 1970s, feminist and liberal democratic ideas of gender equality have also underpinned a great deal of the research into gender and women. In particular, academic and applied studies of economic development have stressed the need to attend to women's roles as producers and providers of food in subsistence-based economies, and the problems that arise when projects involve predominantly male labour. Within anthropology, approaches to gender inequality have varied. In the relativist tradition that has characterised the discipline, many writers stressed complementarity and argued that the use of Western or European ideas of status differentiation were inappropriate and failed to capture cultural ideals of reciprocity and interdependence between the sexes (e.g. O'Brien and Tiffany 1984; Weiner 1976). Annette Weiner's study of Trobriand women (1976) emphasised the differences between men's and women's value and the ways that cultural measures of status were incommensurable with their analogues in Euro-American societies. Margaret Jolly (1994) delineated the ways that distinct domains of power enabled women to gain prestige and status in a Vanuatu society. Lisette Josephides (1985) was one of few feminist anthropologists who attended to the use of physical violence by men to subjugate and gain control over women's productivity for their own ends.

Marilyn Strathern (1980) had argued that women were positioned 'in-between' and so were valued as wives and sisters in different ways. In her later work, she insisted that Eurocentric models of sociality and the individuality of persons inevitably compromised the concepts of inequality employed in analyses of Melanesian gender relations (Strathern 1988). Her theories of Melanesian personhood have had a profound effect on subsequent anthropological research into gender relations (see e.g. Eves 1998; Wardlow 2006).

One of the main arguments of Strathern's work was that the Western notion of individual subjectivity meant that 'a person can dominate another by depriving him or her of that subjectivity' (1988: 338), whereas Melanesian understandings of personhood prevented this form of dominance. She did acknowledge that it is 'harder to understand women's apparent willingness and their seeming connivance in situations that appear to go against their own interests' (339), but insisted that this was because as a 'partible person' a woman embodied the interests of others and so acted in terms of those interests. Her study, while acknowledging social and economic change in Melanesian exchange systems, did not explore the implications of these changes for women's interests in the context of their roles in the modern economy; nor did it deal with contemporary national or provincial politics. This image of the partible person, deliberately presented as an ideal type rather than a contemporary reality, has been criticised as ahistorical, because it clearly ignores the decades of influences and 'encompassment' by 'Western capitalism, Christianity, and commercially driven mass culture' (LiPuma 2000: 5). It perpetuates a distinction of radical alterity between 'Melanesia' and 'the West' that, as Jolly has pointed out, 'leaves out some of the most interesting chapters in the recent history of the region, unwritten chapters replete with gendered personae and processes that constitute exchanges with the "West'" (1992: 146). Such exchanges include the adoption of processes that established political independence and the nationhood of Melanesian countries; the introduction of state institutions such as national education systems and health services; and the economic transformations that linked these nations to the global economy.

In the same year that Strathern's book was published, Paula Brown wrote about the changes that had occurred in women's lives, predicting that more dramatic changes would occur as more women gained education and moved from villages to towns (1988: 137). She foresaw increased participation in political life and consequent gains in equality in employment and public life. Twelve years later, in her book *Changing Gender Relations in Papua New Guinea: The Role of Women's Organisations,* Orovu Sepoe presented a sustained analysis of the ways that women's organisations contributed to the development of strategies for increasing women's political and economic participation. Noting that women continue to have much lower rates of education and employment, she observed that major changes in the lives of both urban and rural woman would be needed. She documented the history and activities of several women's organisations, revealing the various ways such associations have been agents of change in women's lives for many years. Analogous organisations have been at the centre of endeavours to improve the lives of women across the Pacific (George 2012).

As the authors in this collection show, in the decades that followed the initial publication of Strathern's book, dramatic changes occurred that have brought about generational differences, regional variations and introduced new ideas about gender, personhood and women's roles in society. Changes in men's lives, wrought by new forms of employment and new political roles, were particularly associated with rapid urbanisation. New nationhood for previously colonised Melanesia meant that, across the region, urban centres expanded with new employment opportunities. As more men had formal educational qualifications they dominated public and private sectors. But over the following decades many young men moved from village to town hoping to find work and enjoy the excitement of city life, only to find that jobs were scarce. Underemployment of young men and women is now a problem in most Melanesian countries and is associated with rising crime (Dinnen 1993; Kraemer n.d.; Macintyre 2008).

While there is a considerable anthropological literature that documents ideals of masculinity and male activities, as they were enacted in village tribal settings, this genre tends to emphasise initiation, warriorhood and men's activities in exchange rituals. Marilyn Strathern's early study of Highland migrants *No Money on Our Skins* (1975) provides an unsurpassed analysis of the lives of young men who came to Port Moresby in search of work in the 1970s. Only recently have more writers concentrated on the lives of men and gender relations in towns, the ideals and activities of men as they encounter and attempt to manage new inequalities, economic precariousness and changing notions of gender roles (Goddard 2005; Martin 2013; Reed 2003; Taylor 2010, 2016).

In this volume, Stephanie Lusby and Jenny Munro each examine the tensions and problems in men's lives, in Papua New Guinea and West Papua respectively, as they are manifest in urban work environments and in their relations with other men and women in differing contexts. New styles of masculine behaviour associated with employment and educational attainment become markers of class and status as a 'modern' urban person. But, as both authors explain, often men are ambivalent about the concomitant changes in women's lives and they too appeal to gendered distinctions that they locate in 'tradition' or 'custom'. They can resort to violence as a way of 'disciplining' or punishing wives and women who do not conform to the normative values or behaviours that they consider appropriate. But as Munro illustrates, even a man who does hit his wife is aware that this is unacceptable. As he struggles with racism, poverty, dashed hopes and an acute awareness of contemporary inequalities generated by the Indonesian state, he recognises the value of gender equality.

While anthropologists engaged in debates about the nature of gender relations and the problems of applying Western notions of status and oppression to Melanesian societies, within development studies there was little doubt that the lives of women needed to change for the better. The arguments of aid agencies such as UNIFEM and AusAID concentrated on ways of advancing women's interests in economic development and increasing women's participation in education, employment and politics. From the 1980s almost all aid donors and non-government organisations acknowledged that gender initiatives aimed at including women had to be incorporated into economic development and aid projects. High maternal and infant mortality; the scourges of malaria, tuberculosis and HIV/AIDS; low rates of education for girls and few opportunities for women to engage in income-generating projects were problems that demanded changes in the ways that aid projects were designed and implemented. The strong cultural relativism of anthropology that inhibited researchers from characterising Melanesian women as oppressed or in need of assistance in engaging with modernity never really had much purchase among aid project practitioners. They held much more to ideas of economic advancement and modernisation and emphasised the need for gender equity and inclusiveness in development projects (Stratigos and Hughes (eds) 1987; United Nations 1996).

Twenty years on, 15 years after ambitious Millennium Development Goals were set for changes in gender equality across the Pacific, the gains have not been dramatic—but there have been gains. This volume documents and analyses some of the changes that Melanesian women have experienced and the many ways that they are initiating changes for themselves. It also shows how many of the old debates about the tensions between 'tradition' and 'modernity' persist in contemporary discourses surrounding gender relations. The hopes and aspirations of young women, especially those who have gained education in the last decade, are now finding expression in ways that have no precedent in the Pacific. Where in the past women's organisations often willingly confined their interests to 'women's issues' and did not challenge the male dominance of political institutions or access to employment, young women are now raising the issues in a variety of contexts (see Spark 2014a, 2015). They are mindful of the strengths of Melanesian women who are their forebears, metaphorically and actually (see Rooney, this volume), but they are also prepared to challenge the restrictions of earlier gender ideals.

I have worked in Papua New Guinea for almost 40 years and much of my research and practical engagement on a variety of projects has concentrated on women's lives and gender relations (Macintyre 1998). When, in 1979, I first undertook fieldwork on the island of Tubetube in Milne Bay Province, I was impressed by the commitment to girls' education and optimistic about the future of those who gained entry to secondary school from the small community school on the island. They had role models from the late 1960s, when several young Tubetube women had completed high school and gained tertiary qualifications and well-paid jobs in journalism, dentistry and clerical administration (Macintyre 1985). The experiences of the following generation revealed the difficulties they faced; difficulties echoed in the lives of many of their contemporaries elsewhere in Papua New Guinea. Parents could not pay fees; homesickness and the problems of adjusting to boarding-school life caused girls to drop out; one girl became pregnant, another lost interest in her studies—none of them followed the examples of their predecessors. These girls returned to the island, married and followed in their mothers' footsteps, becoming skilled gardeners and bearers of children. While at first some referred to themselves shamefacedly as 'dropouts' they have all adapted to life on this small island with equanimity. But all harbour hopes that their children will gain an education that will enable them to move to town and find a job that pays well.

In 1995 I undertook a study of the possible social impacts of a large gold mine in Lihir, an island off the coast of New Ireland in Papua New Guinea. Before the mining operations began the people were subsistence gardeners, and I observed levels of rural poverty beyond those I had seen in Milne Bay Province. There were relatively few ways that people could make money and the travel to commercial centres was difficult. Not surprisingly, most Lihirians welcomed the mine as an opportunity for economic advancement. They negotiated an Integrated Benefits Package with the mining company that gave privileged access to jobs, a housing scheme, a road around the island, royalties, new schools and a hospital. At that time nobody on the island imagined that the negative effects might ever outweigh these benefits, and women I interviewed were enthusiastic supporters of the project. Many women were eager to gain employment.

At the time construction of the mine began, Lihirian women had high hopes of employment and were quite adventurous about the sorts of jobs they might take on. But with the exception of the few who trained as heavy vehicle drivers (see Macintyre 2001) most were employed in positions that reflected mining company policies—as cleaners, laundry workers and clerical staff. Part of the training for female staff included sessions on grooming, applying make-up and nail polish and 'feminine comportment'. The global mining industry is overwhelmingly masculine and its hiring policies everywhere reflect gendered stereotypes of workers. Women in secretarial and clerical positions were well paid, but the majority of women earned extremely low wages. During the 10 years I worked in Lihir only one woman was appointed as a supervisor and not one held a managerial position.

While I experienced disappointment at the ways that gender disparities, inequalities in the workplace and Western assumptions about the sexual division of labour were instituted in Lihir, most of the female employees did not. In interviews conducted each year, the majority of women employees said that their economic independence outweighed other problems (Macintyre 2011). But given that the resources boom in Papua New Guinea has meant that similar employment policies have been established in every mine site, the forces of economic globalisation can only be seen as conservative in respect to gender and work. Across the Pacific, particularly in countries where the dominant industries involve the exploitation of natural resources by foreign companies, men gain more jobs than women. Their employers often implicitly reinforce values of male economic privilege that affect familial relations and marginalise women.

Stephanie Lusby's chapter in this volume illustrates the ways that Melanesian men working in the security industry construe violence, including domestic violence, as a masculine prerogative. She shows also that contemporary aspirational masculine behaviour embodies ethical considerations that justify violence when it is used to enforce discipline and actions that are 'right'. This moral justification, which people perceive as both traditional and Christian, affirms gendered behaviours and positions men as the arbiters and instruments of punishment. Munro's chapter recounts the use of violence by a West Papuan husband who, in the context of stigmatising racism, discrimination and economic disadvantage, struggles to live up to his own ideals of gender equality.

The tensions that girls and women experience as they attempt to embrace aspects of modernity through education and employment are not new, but the numbers of women affected across the Pacific are increasing. Dramatic differences have occurred through communications technology. Mobile phones and computers are ubiquitous in towns; and even in places as remote as Tubetube several people have them.

Tait Brimacombe (this volume) demonstrates how these forms of communication enable new ways of participating in actions that are both social and political. The formation of groups on Facebook and other social media sites not only links people with shared interests and political concerns, it also enables them to express opinions and respond to political actions. Civil society organisations have flourished in the last decade and the emergence of organisations such as Pacific Young Women's Leadership Alliance facilitates communication across the region. As Brimacombe reveals, sponsored conferences bring together young women whose shared visions of new social and political roles challenge the sexism and parochialism of the past. In considering the mechanisms of 'transition' in a complex, contemporary context, the young women who participate in conversations within and between these broadly based organisations provide striking examples of new initiatives. Their adoption of electronic media has been one of the more remarkable changes in the ways that women can form communities of interest.

I recall when people first began using computers in Lihir. During their lunch hour young women would surf the web, usually looking for evangelical Christian sites. But over time their interests have become more diverse, and they now use Facebook, often following newsfeeds and discussions that are concerned with issues in Papua New Guinea and the Pacific. Websites where women can debate, join forces, protest and respond to social injustices now abound. Often men participate in conversations on these sites dealing with gender relations and female disadvantage. Frequently the tenor is feminist or progressive in tone, with people decrying violence and endorsing changes that will enable women to participate in economic and political activities.

There are two significant changes in the ways that women now voice their views when compared with conversations a decade ago. First, many are extraordinarily confident. Second, they regularly appeal to the notion of human rights. As the authors in this collection observe, even when women are uncertain of their rights defined by international conventions or in the constitution or laws of their countries, they regularly invoke human rights as they protest or describe various disadvantages (Jolly 2000; Macintyre 2000). In the mid-1990s, while conducting consultations with people in urban centres across Papua New Guinea, many people, both male and female, professed ignorance of the meaning of the term. Sometimes one or two people rejected the idea that human rights were relevant to Papua New Guineans, some stating baldly that these were for 'white people' and 'against custom'. As Pauline Soaki (this volume) observes, there are still many who express reservations about the relationship between customs or tradition and the idea that people, individually or collectively, have rights. But in the intervening years, as non-government organisations, foreign aid donors, churches and local groups have invoked the idea of human rights in the context of gender equality, it has become a central theme in campaigns (Macintyre 2000: 167).

The role of international agencies in promoting a discourse of human rights was boosted during the Decade for Women (1975–1986), and women from Pacific countries attended the United Nations conferences in Mexico City, Nairobi and Beijing as representatives of women's organisations. The governments of Fiji, Solomon Islands, Vanuatu and Papua New Guinea are all signatories to the Convention on the Elimination of All Forms of Discrimination against Women (CEDAW), but in practice many of the aims of that convention are ignored or neglected (Biersack, Jolly and Macintyre (eds) 2016). That said, the appeal to human rights is increasingly made by Melanesian women's organisations in their own terms as they define the issues that affect their lives. Throughout the region, groups defined as 'civil society' organisations have gained strength and in many respects appear to have had greater success in mobilising women's grassroots support. Funding, training and administrative reinforcement from foreign aid agencies has assisted in the growth of organisations such as the Fiji Women's Crisis Centre, the Vanuatu Women's Centre and analogous bodies that support campaigns aimed at improving women's lives.

The campaigns, alas, are generally around issues identified 30 years ago: women's health; difficulties of access to education; discriminatory work practices; and violence against women. In recent years, the killings associated with sorcery accusations in Papua New Guinea can been added to the litany of social problems that disproportionately affect women. In all Melanesian countries, violence against women remains common and condoned. Whereas in places such as Australia and the United States (where rates also continue to be appallingly high), domestic violence is now stigmatised and unequivocally criminalised, across the Pacific it is contentiously linked to ideologies of male entitlement and authority and practices such as bride price payment (Macintyre 2012). As Soaki found in her study, many Melanesian women continue to condone marital violence as legitimate punishment for a wife's misbehaviour. The perennial debate over whether such social ills should be attributed to the dramatic changes associated with modernity, or whether they are contemporary manifestations of attitudes and behaviours that existed in the distant past, continues to dominate discussions.

But the changes in gender relations since colonisation, and in ways of life more generally, ensure that what counts as 'tradition' is often quite different from past constructions of customary practices and values. As the chapters in this volume show, the appeals to custom, as well as the decrying of its effects, now incorporate Christian ideals of marriage, accommodate new patterns of employment and certainly adhere to entirely different dress codes from those that prevailed in any Melanesian precolonial past (see Spark 2014a, 2014b, 2015). Across the Pacific region, the enveloping Mother Hubbard dresses introduced by nineteenth-century missionaries to cover bare legs and breasts are now considered 'traditional' and worn with pride as 'national dress' (Jolly 2014). Young women who wear tight-fitting garments or trousers are considered immodest and older people lament the influence of Western fashions. Indeed, the contemporary 'sartorial struggle' (Jolly 2014: 450) encapsulates not only debates over appropriately modest comportment by women, but it is also considered the clear indication of changing sexual mores that threaten gender hierarchies and contribute to epidemics such as HIV/AIDS (Cummings 2008).

External markers such as clothing are interpreted also as indicators of deeper changes in values and social roles. This generation of young people across Melanesia has perhaps been more exposed to different ideas of marriage and the role of women in the family than any previously (Spark 2011). The ideals of Christian, companionate marriage introduced by missionaries in the nineteenth and early twentieth centuries have taken hold in some quarters, but not others. Recent evangelical churches have promoted models of the nuclear family and household that emphasise more individualistic social values (Cox and Macintyre 2014; Maggio 2016). As Jenny Munro, Ceridwen Spark and John Cox show in this volume, there is greater acceptance of the value of women's education and even the view that having a working wife might be an advantage rather than a threat. But the variations across the region and within each country mean that generalisations about the progress of these emergent patterns are difficult to make.

Education is highly valued as a means to social mobility and employment, and over the past 20 years the gender balance has improved at every educational level. In Fiji and Vanuatu, all children now attend primary school, in Solomon Islands 87 per cent attend, while Papua New Guinea lags at 63 per cent (UNESCO 2015). In his chapter, John Cox presents a Solomon Islands kindergarten as an example of the way that gender inequalities in education are being challenged at the grassroots level. In North Vella, women established a kindergarten and the woman who initiated the project was strongly supported by her husband. He demonstrates how gender ideologies can be challenged indirectly through projects emphasising the value of education for all children.

Spark, in her study of young women in Port Vila and Port Moresby, considers the ways that their education affects their lives and values. She maintains that 'women's education and employment enables them to exercise new-found decision-making power with regard to their intimate relationships' (Spark, this volume). She explores the attitudes and aspirations of tertiary-educated women who earn sufficient money to be financially independent and finds that their ideas of love, marriage and family constitute a radical departure from the norms and values of rural women. Their financial autonomy affords them greater freedom, not only as consumers, but in a wide range of social contexts. This perhaps is the sort of change that Paula Brown envisaged in 1988.

Reflecting on my own encounters with Melanesian women over several decades, the transformations documented and analysed in this collection are in some respects unsurprising. They have been in process for several decades and the capacity of Melanesian people to adopt, adapt and forge changes in their lives has long been remarked upon. When I first went to Papua New Guinea, I was convinced that those changes would proceed at a rapid pace. The heady period around independence seemed to usher in an optimism and a pervasive sense of opportunity and possibility. In 1977, when the first election after independence saw Nahau Rooney, Waliyato Clowes and Josephine Abaijah elected, I expected that the number of women in Papua New Guinea's parliament would gradually increase. It declined. After independence, I thought that women were ensconced in senior public service positions; currently they occupy roughly the same number of senior posts as they did in 1980. The problems that women face in gaining managerial positions seem not to have abated. Rather, they have become more complicated as more young people find that there are simply not enough jobs to fulfil their dreams of permanent, salaried positions, and life in towns brings new problems of housing and economic precariousness. While some young men and women who find paid work flourish, creating new social networks and embracing new ideals of love and marriage, others find themselves marginalised by modernity.

Melanesian social worlds are in flux. While there is increasing engagement in various entrepreneurial activities, in many places this is inflected by older social relationships that oblige people to share and redistribute any gains. Employment associated with mining and fishing has increased, but the workforce is overwhelmingly male. Teaching and nursing still attract women who see them as nurturant professions, consonant with accepted female dispositions. But there are now women who are engineers, geologists and chemists, and many women work in the commercial sector in towns. The social and cultural changes in gender relations occur in the context of growing participation in the global economy and the expansion of communication technologies. There are new inequalities and struggles as people adjust and adapt to new circumstances. The chapters in this volume contribute to knowledge and understanding of the effects of this flux on gender relations.

References

Biersack, Aletta, Margaret Jolly and Martha Macintyre (eds). 2016. *Gender Violence and Human Rights: Seeking Justice in Fiji, Papua New Guinea and Vanuatu*. Canberra: ANU Press.

Brown, Paula. 1988. 'Gender and social change: New forms of independence for Simbu women'. *Oceania* 59(2): 123–42. doi. org/10.1002/j.1834-4461.1988.tb02315.x.

Butt, Leslie and Richard Eves (eds). 2008. *Making Sense of AIDS: Culture, Sexuality and Power in Melanesia*. Honolulu: University of Hawai'i Press.

Choi, Hyaeweol and Margaret Jolly (eds). 2014. *Divine Domesticities: Christian Paradoxes in Asia and the Pacific*. Canberra: ANU Press. Online: press.anu.edu.au/publications/divine-domesticities (accessed 11 August 2016).

Convention on the Elimination of All Forms of Discrimination against Women (CEDAW). 1979. *UN Women*. Online: www. un.org/womenwatch/daw/cedaw/text/econvention.htm (accessed 11 December 2014).

Cox, John and Martha Macintyre. 2014. 'Christian marriage, money scams, and Melanesian social imaginaries'. *Oceania* 84(2): 138–57. doi.org/10.1002/ocea.5048.

Cummings, Maggie. 2008. 'The trouble with trousers: Gossip, *kastom* and sexual culture in Vanuatu'. In *Making Sense of AIDS: Culture, Sexuality and Power in Melanesia*, ed. Leslie Butt and Richard Eves, pp. 132–49. Honolulu: University of Hawai'i Press. doi.org/10.21313/ hawaii/9780824831936.003.0008.

Dickson-Waiko, Anne. 2010. 'Taking over, of what and from whom? Women and independence, the PNG experience'. The Alfred Deakin Research Institute, Working Papers, no. 10.

Dinnen, Sinclair. 1993. 'Big men, small men and invisible women—urban crime and inequality in Papua New Guinea'. *Australian and New Zealand Journal of Criminology* 26(1): 19–34. doi.org/10.1177/000486589302600104.

Douglas, Bronwen. 2003. 'Christianity, tradition and everyday modernity: Towards an anatomy of women's groupings in Melanesia'. *Oceania* 74(1–2): 6–23. doi.org/10.1002/j.1834-4461.2003.tb02833.x.

Eves, Richard. 1998. *The Magical Body: Power, Fame and Meaning in a Melanesian Society*. Reading: Harwood Academic Publishers.

George, Nicole. 2012. *Situating Women: Gender Politics and Circumstance in Fiji*. Canberra: ANU E Press. Online: press.anu.edu.au/publications/situating-women (accessed 11 August 2016).

Goddard, Michael. 2005. *The Unseen City Anthropological Perspectives on Port Moresby, Papua New Guinea*. Canberra: Pandanus Books.

Hilsdon, Anne-Marie, Martha Macintyre, Vera Mackie and Maila Stivens (eds). 2000. *Human Rights and Gender Politics: Perspectives on the Asia-Pacific Region*. London: Routledge.

Inter-Parliamentary Union for Democracy. 2015. *Women in Parliament, 20 Years in Review*. Geneva.

Jolly, Margaret. 2014. 'A saturated history of Christianity and cloth in Oceania'. In *Divine Domesticities: Christian Paradoxes in Asia and the Pacific*, ed. Hyaeweol Choi and Margaret Jolly, pp. 429–54. Canberra: ANU Press. Online: press.anu.edu.au/publications/divine-domesticities (accessed 11 August 2016).

——. 2000. '*Woman ikat raet long human raet o no?* Women's rights, human rights and domestic violence in Vanuatu'. In *Human Rights and Gender Politics: Perspectives on the Asia-Pacific Region*, ed. Anne-Marie Hilsdon, Martha Macintyre, Vera Mackie and Maila Stivens, pp. 124–46. London: Routledge.

——. 1994. *Women of the Place: Kastom, Colonialism, and Gender in Vanuatu*. Philadelphia: Harwood Academic Publishers.

——. 1992. 'Partible persons and multiple authors'. [Contribution to Book Review Forum on Marilyn Strathern's *The Gender of the Gift*]. *Pacific Studies* 15(1): 137–49.

Jolly, Margaret and Martha Macintyre (eds). 1989. *Family and Gender in the Pacific: Domestic Contradictions and the Colonial Impact.* Cambridge: Cambridge University Press.

Jolly, Margaret, Christine Stewart with Carolyn Brewer (eds). 2012. *Engendering Violence in Papua New Guinea.* Canberra: ANU E Press. Online: press.anu.edu.au/publications/engendering-violence-papua-new-guinea (accessed 11 August 2016).

Josephides, Lisette. 1985. *The Production of Inequality: Gender and Exchange among the Kewa.* London: Tavistock.

Kraemer, Daniela. n.d. *'Now I Can See' Thoughts of some Boys in Port Vila Town* (film).

LiPuma, Edward. 2000. *Encompassing Others: The Magic of Modernity in Melanesia.* Ann Arbor: University of Michigan Press.

Macintyre, Martha. 2012. 'Gender violence in Melanesia and the problem of Millennium Development Goal No. 3'. In *Engendering Violence in Papua New Guinea*, ed. Margaret Jolly, Christine Stewart with Carolyn Brewer, pp. 239–66. Canberra: ANU E Press. Online: press.anu.edu.au/publications/engendering-violence-papua-new-guinea (accessed 11 August 2016).

——. 2011. 'Money changes everything. Papua New Guinean women in the modern economy'. In *Managing Modernity in the Western Pacific*, ed. Mary Patterson and Martha Macintyre, pp. 90–120. St Lucia: University of Queensland Press.

——. 2008. 'Police and thieves, gunmen and drunks: Problems with men and problems with society in Papua New Guinea'. In *Changing Pacific Masculinities*, ed. John P. Taylor. Special issue: *The Australian Journal of Anthropology* 19(2): 179–93.

——. 2001. 'Taking care of culture: Consultancy, anthropology and gender issues'. *Social Analysis* 45(2): 108–19.

——. 2000. '"Hear us, women of Papua New Guinea": Melanesian women and human rights'. In *Human Rights and Gender Politics: Perspectives on the Asia-Pacific Region*, ed. Anne-Marie Hilsdon, Martha Macintyre, Vera Mackie and Maila Stivens, pp. 147–71. London: Routledge.

——. 1998. 'The persistence of inequality: Women in Papua New Guinea since independence'. In *Modern Papua New Guinea*, ed. Laura Zimmer-Tamakoshi, pp. 211–31. Kirksville, MS: Thomas Jefferson University Press.

——. 1985. 'Women and local politics on Tubetube, Milne Bay Province'. *Women in Politics in Papua New Guinea*. Working Paper No. 6, Department of Political and Social Change, Research School Pacific Studies, The Australian National University, pp. 19–25.

Maggio, Rodolfo. 2016. '"My wife converted me": Gendered values and gendered conversion in Pentecostal households in Honiara, Solomon Islands'. In *Gender and Christianity in Melanesia: Towards a Unified Analysis*, ed. Michelle MacCarthy and Annelin Eriksen. Special issue: *The Australian Journal of Anthropology* 27(2): 168–84. doi. org/10.1111/taja.12192.

Martin, Keir. 2013. *The Death of the Big Men and the Rise of the Big Shots: Custom and Conflict in East New Britain*. New York: Berghahn Books.

McDougall, Debra. 2003. 'Fellowship and citizenship as models of national community: United Church Women's fellowship in Ranongga, Solomon Islands'. *Oceania* 74(1–2): 61–80. doi. org/10.1002/j.1834-4461.2003.tb02836.x.

O'Brien, Denise and Sharon Tiffany. 1984. *Rethinking Women's Roles: Perspectives from the Pacific*. Berkeley: University of California Press.

Pacific Women in Politics (PACWIP) n.d. Website. Online: www.pacwip. org (accessed 20 June 2016).

Patterson, Mary and Martha Macintyre (eds). 2011. *Managing Modernity in the Western Pacific*. St Lucia: University of Queensland Press.

Pollard, Alice Aruhe'eta and Marilyn Waring (eds). 2010. *Being the First: Storis blong oloketa mere lo Solomon Aelan*. Honiara: Pacific Media Centre for the Institute of Public Policy and Regional Assistance Mission to Solomon Islands (RAMSI).

Reed, Adam. 2003. *Papua New Guinea's Last Place: Experiences of Constraint in a Postcolonial Prison*. New York: Berghan.

Sepoe, Orovu V. 2000. *Changing Gender Relations in Papua New Guinea: The Role of Women's Organisations*. New Delhi: UBS Publishers.

Spark, Ceridwen. 2015. '"Working out what to wear": The politics of fashion in *Stella*'. *The Contemporary Pacific* 27(1): 39–70. doi. org/10.1353/cp.2015.0019.

——. 2014a. 'An Oceanic revolution? *Stella* and the construction of new femininities in Papua New Guinea and the Pacific'. *The Australian Journal of Anthropology* 25(1): 54–72. doi.org/10.1111/taja.12066.

——. 2014b. '"We only get the daylight hours": Gender, fear and freedom in urban Papua New Guinea'. *Security Challenges* 10(2): 15–31.

——. 2011. 'Gender trouble in town: Educated women eluding male domination, gender violence and marriage in PNG'. *The Asia Pacific Journal of Anthropology* 12(2): 164–80. doi.org/10.1080/14442213.2 010.546425.

Strathern, Marilyn. 1988. *The Gender of the Gift: Problems with Women and Problems with Society in Melanesia*. Berkeley: University of California Press. doi.org/10.1525/california/9780520064232.001.0001.

——. 1980. *Women in Between. Female Roles in a Male World: Mount Hagen, New Guinea*. London: Seminar Press.

——. 1975. *No Money on Our Skins: Migrants in Port Moresby*. New Guinea Research Unit, The Australian National University, Canberra.

Stratigos, Susan and Philip J. Hughes (eds). 1987. *Women as Unequal Partners in Development*. Australian International Development Assistance Bureau. Women in Development Fund. Port Moresby: University of Papua New Guinea.

Taylor, John Patrick. 2016. 'Drinking money and pulling women: Mobile phone talk, gender, and agency in Vanuatu'. *Anthropological Forum* 26(1): 1–16. doi.org/10.1080/00664677.2015.1071238.

——. 2010. 'Janus and the siren's call: Kava and the articulation of gender and modernity in Vanuatu'. *Journal of the Royal Anthropological Institute* 16(2): 279–96. doi.org/10.1111/j.1467-9655.2010.01625.x.

Turner, Ann. 1993. *Views from Interviews: The Changing Role of Women in PNG*. Melbourne: Oxford University Press.

United Nations. 1996. *The United Nations and the Advancement of Women, 1945–1996.* New York: Department of Public Information. Online: www.mdgmonitor.org/mdg-3-promote-gender-equality-and-empower-women/ (accessed 11 August 2016).

United Nations Children's Fund. n.d. 'Papua New Guinea: Activities'. Online: www.unicef.org/png/activities_4369.html (accessed 20 June 2016).

United Nations Educational, Scientific and Cultural Organization (UNESCO). 2015. *Pacific Education for All 2015 Review.* Apia: UNESCO, Office for the Pacific States.

Wardlow, Holly. 2006. *Wayward Women: Sexuality and Agency in a New Guinea Society.* Berkeley: University of California Press.

Weiner, Annette. 1976. *Women of Value, Men of Renown.* Austin: University of Texas Press.

1

Securitisation, development and the invisibility of gender

Stephanie Lusby

The Australian National University

Introduction

Discussions of violence are ubiquitous in, and with regard to, Papua New Guinea. In this chapter, I discuss how persistent broader contexts of legitimised violence shape efforts to destabilise particular patterns of violence, namely, male violence against women. Looking at the perspectives of men working in the security industry in PNG, I argue that the increased traction and centrality of discourses of securitisation in the name of national development allows violence against men accused of criminal or anti-social behaviour to persist. Critically, the silences around the gendered dimensions of violence between men excused as 'disciplinary' produces double standards that are unhelpful to efforts to improve gender equality. Here, I seek to illustrate that narratives of discipline and security form a continuum in discussions of violence, highlighting the need for politicised and holistic approaches to gender in violence interventions.

Violence frames development policy in significant ways. It directly impacts on the quality of life of victims of crime and those who fear being victims (Goldstein 2010; Lakhani and Willman 2014). Within contemporary discourses of development, public violence is further represented as a threat to foreign investment, economic growth and the country's future, as well as the stability and growth of the region (Dinnen and Mcleod 2008; Lakhani and Willman 2014; Scott 2005). Within these framings, which are predicated on notions of state security, the bolstering of the capacity of law and order agencies to respond to crime is of primary concern. Immediate responses either by state agents or by private security firms acting alongside or even in proxy for police often involve violence being made legitimate through its purpose of improving security and therefore community well-being.

Responses to violence against women, particularly private violence that occurs in homes and by people otherwise known to the victim, is framed in slightly different ways. Although improving police and court responses are critical here too, public awareness campaigns focus more on shifting social norms that deny women's rights to bodily autonomy, safety, and equal access to justice. Broadly speaking, within frameworks of securitisation, punishment and disciplinary action are foregrounded with the aim of deterring others from enacting violent crime. Rights-based approaches have a different emphasis, giving greater attention to prevention strategies aimed at changing men's behaviour and encouraging broader attitudinal change with regard to the rights and roles of men and women. Whether talking about public or private violence, however, men are more likely to be the perpetrators of violence, whether as street criminals, referred to as *raskols*, as security agents, or as domestic assailants. Men are the key targets, then, of both approaches to crime response and prevention.

Programs built along each strategy are designed to work in concert and complementarity: adequate law enforcement responses to family and sexual violence, for example, are critical to precipitating behaviour change (CIMC and FSVAC n.d.; Klugman et al. 2014; Merry 2006). However, while the gendered dimensions of violence against women by men are central to those discussions, they are almost invisible in mainstream discussions of securitisation. Violence between men as *raskols*, and predominately men as security and police, is just violence; the gendered contours of those interactions are rarely scrutinised.

In this chapter, I endeavour to unpack the gendered character of violence between men, and how the logic applied to expressions of aggression done in the name of discipline and security intersects with anti-violence against women initiatives. How do men narrate violence against men that is done in the name of social control? And what does that mean for how they narrate violence against women? I argue that the gendered meanings of violence committed as a result of criminal or anti-social activity, and excessive force against citizens used in the name of social order and security is ostensibly the same; that both are articulations of aggressive masculinity. As Sally Engle Merry reminds us, 'While violence exists in a culture-free zone of injury and death, it's meanings are deeply informed by social contexts' (Merry 2006: 24). These meanings allow violence to be interpreted as either legitimate or illegitimate. Thus the broad acceptance of disciplinary violence between men in the name of 'security' undermines attempts to destabilise excuses for male violence against women that rest upon sexist logic of women's need to be disciplined by men, and their morals and bodies policed.

I explore these issues through considering the perspectives of entry-level security guards in Kokopo, East New Britain. Over a three-month period in 2012, I conducted weekly discussion groups with between 10 and 30 men working as guards. Their perspectives are critical to understanding how different development discourses about violence and its legitimacy are hybridised and gendered. This is because of what the security industry represents within the political economy of Papua New Guinea's development, and what they can tell us about how this affects the personhood of young men engaged in security work.

Violence and the security industry

The security industry is hugely important in Papua New Guinea. Concerns about safety, crime and the capacity of law and order agencies to respond are not novel in PNG. However, in the almost two decades since securitisation for development became a dominant narrative globally, and for PNG and its donor partners (Goldstein 2010; O'Connor, Chan and Goodman 2006; Scott 2005), security companies have been relied upon increasingly to fill lacunae in state capacity (Dinnen 2001; Lakhani and Willman 2014; SIA 2014). In 2006, there were 173 firms registered with the SIA (Security Industries Association, after 2014 Security Industries Authority). As of December 2013, there were 470 registered companies and 24,000 guards, and more suspected of operating unregistered (limited staff capacity within SIA prohibits accurate monitoring of all companies across the country) (private discussion with Paul Kingston Asari, 28 August 2014).

On their website, the SIA theorises about the growth of the security industry, writing that it is partly due to 'the insufficient manpower in the law enforcement agencies to meet the basic security needs of the 7 million PNG citizens. Consequently licensed private security companies are taking advantages of this to fill the vacuum to perform quasi law enforcement duties' (SIA 2014). A recent World Bank survey of the social and economic costs of violence in PNG found that many business houses 'acknowledged that they hired private security to help secure their premises, but also often turned to private security in lieu of the police in the event of an incident' (Lakhani and Willman 2014: 9). However, security guards are not hired for the protection of the community at large, but are for-profit companies designed to protect the particular interests of those who engage their services and whose business growth depends on a continuing sense of insecurity from those who can afford to pay for security services. In the same World Bank study, some respondents reported suspicions that:

> private security companies may also create 'security incidents' by staging an attack on a business premises. This, allegedly, is done in order to create demand for their services or to undermine their competitors (Lakhani and Willman 2014: 10).

The rise in security has coincided with a depreciation of confidence in state policing. In 2012, there were 184 police stations across PNG, including posts of only one or two officers, and 5,387 uniformed officers, only 623 of whom were women (Papua New Guinea–Australia Law and Justice Partnership 2013). Many Papua New Guineans have an ambivalent relationship with police, with accusations that the law 'lacks teeth'—that is, does not pose adequate risk of punishment to criminals so as to deter crime, and excessive use of force and police brutality are both commonly reported complaints (Akmeemana et al. 2014; Human Rights Watch 2005). With regard to the former, limited staff numbers impinge on responses to call outs. This is compounded with poor investigative capacity at many stations, which, in turn, impacts on whether complaints will progress to arrest or court hearings (Dinnen 2001). 'Emergency responses' to suspected 'gang' or *raskol* crime by police often involve brutal raids on settlement areas accused of harbouring criminals. Police violence—during raids, arrests and when detainees are incarcerated in police stations—is reportedly common (Human Rights Watch 2015).

Although not unproblematised, there are also widely held public perceptions that 'something must be done' to address crime in PNG, and there is a political onus to be tough on crime. Despite some observers noting that, rather than resolving issues of criminal violence, police raids in Port Moresby, for example, in fact seem to exacerbate problems (Dinnen 2001), tacit acceptance of some degree of police violence is widely prevalent in media and public discourse across the country. Grudgingly permissive attitudes towards institutional violence are reinforced by narratives of securitisation and public fear, but also validate the notoriously macho cultures within the Royal Papua New Guinea Constabulary (RPNGC). Despite institutional efforts to elicit change through gender sensitivity and operational training (Macintyre 2012; Mcleod and Macintyre 2010), such attitudes remain pervasive and continue to perpetuate aggressive masculinity within the force, resulting in human rights abuses against men, women and children accused of committing or being complicit in crimes (Amnesty International 2006; Human Rights Watch 2005, 2015).

These same philosophies and practices have translated into the operations of security personnel. However, as 'quasi-law enforcement', security guards are not privy to the same levels of training, public scrutiny or regulation as state services. Even though such checks and balances are often shown to be inadequate, and change is slow within the police force, protocols still exist and fall under the purview of government and donor analysis. There is no standardised training curriculum or institution in Papua New Guinea for security guards. The SIA dedicates a section on their website appealing to industry members to help to establish a private college, noting that such an institution is a requirement under the *Security Protection Act* (Independent State of Papua New Guinea 2004). The website notes that because guards currently receive only ad-hoc training, 'all the security guards currently employed in the industry are either not trained or insufficiently trained'. The site goes on to say that:

> the establishment of a private security academy is very important to our long term interest to urgently up skill, rehabilitate and empower the security guards so they are controlled and well disciplined to provide quality services to the services receivers. By doing this all bad habits and serious allegations will be reduced and the integrity of the industry will be maintained (SIA 2014).

The 'bad habits and serious allegations' are indeed cause for concern. There have been several high-profile cases of crimes committed by security guards in PNG that have recently received international attention. Barrick

Gold paid compensation in an out-of-court settlement to 11 of 200 women raped by security personnel hired by the company at Porgera Mine (McVeigh 2015). Australian and Papua New Guinean security guards at the Australian-controlled Manus Island Processing Facility were found to be culpable for violent assaults on asylum seekers in February 2014 (Davey 2014). Australian and Papua New Guinean security guards at the Manus Island facility were found to be unregistered with the SIA at the time of the 2014 riots, where security guards were found responsible for the death of asylum seeker Reza Berati (Wolfe 2014).[1] Other stories of everyday assaults by guards against citizens are occasionally reported in local news media, and regularly appear on social media sites. The World Bank study found that, although use of firearms by security personnel is restricted under the *Security Protection Act*, police weapons were found to be in use by some guards (Lakhani and Willman 2014: 10). Poor regulatory capacity of the SIA means that addressing assaults or misconduct committed by security personnel relies on internal disciplinary measures, or victims being able to report crimes to police and having police respond. As a result, the macho posturing and violence that is enacted by police under the guise of social protection is also perpetuated throughout the security industry, arguably in less visible and more pervasive ways.

Daniel Goldstein observes that the meaning of 'security' is entirely reliant on that which is defined as a threat (2010). The line between categories in Papua New Guinea is slippery and subjective, as responses to anti-social threats in the form of criminal or alleged criminal activity from security forces can be as much a source of uncertainty and fear for communities as the behaviour of *raskols*. Nonetheless, the pervasive fear of violence generally, and its anticipated ill-effects on economic development in particular, means that despite its issues, security remains a growth industry. Consequently, in the small formal employment market in

---

1   The Manus Island Processing Centre has been a contentious issue within PNG, as well as in Australia, since reopening in 2012. The encounters between local youths and notorious PNG Mobile Squad officers, brought in as additional security to Manus Island when the centre reopened, resulted in at least one death (Callinan 2013). There have been ongoing allegations of unequal treatment of local and ex-patriot security guards, with local guards receiving limited training, and reporting poor working conditions. Elected representatives of Manus Island have repeatedly stated that the promised benefits to Manus Islanders, in terms of jobs and inputs into local economies, have not materialised and have been outweighed by negative impacts from the processing centre. The Supreme Court of Papua New Guinea ruled that the Manus facility was unconstitutional in April 2016 (Anderson 2016). At the time of writing, conditions of the closure have not been finalised.

PNG (Pacific Economic Monitor 2014), it is also a significant employer, especially of young men. In the next section, I consider who the guards are and how they discuss threats and acts of security in their own experiences.

Raskols and concerned citizens

How would you translate 'violent man' to Tok Pisin?

Man bilong pait, man nogut—em tok nogut, bikhet man [a fighter, a no-good man—he swears and insults people, he's a big head] … no discipline.

Group discussion with Kokopo Security Guards, 19 September 2012

The composition of the security industry in PNG is diverse. On the one hand, there are the large multinational corporations such as G4S and Transfield Services employing or contracting salaried, trained and armed guards to protect their clients' people and assets. On the other, there are the under-trained and poorly paid guards—sometimes working for the same companies, or for smaller, local firms—who are a common and conspicuous presence in urban areas and resource enclaves. The guards who participated in this research were employed by a locally owned company, whose operations were based mostly in East New Britain as well as contracting out to other parts of the country. Most of the regular guards (as opposed to operations and staff managers) were paid around minimum wage, which at the time of the research was K2.20 (US$0.45) per hour. They worked one week on, during which time they stayed at the company barracks in Kokopo Town, and then had a week off where they were able to go back to their home villages. The company owner described this as a deliberate policy to allow staff to tend to their family and community commitments, but some guards said that working part-time made it difficult to earn enough money to support themselves.

Most of the guards were Tolai from East New Britain, with a small number of men who identified as indigenous minorities from other parts of the province. Some men were migrants from neighbouring West New Britain, New Ireland and mainland provinces. Others were part of the Sepik and Highlands diaspora whose families had settled in East New Britain decades before, or were of mixed Papua New Guinean ethnicity. Although many of the Tolai guards demonstrated generally discriminatory attitudes against *waira*, strangers, this was not outwardly directed against their work mates with whom they had a shared identity as members of the company. The majority of guards were men who had left school at Grade 8 or earlier, usually because of problems with finding the school fees necessary to continue. Many had poor literacy skills and struggled to engage paid work outside of the security sector. They had some access to land but found it difficult to make a living from it, and complained of land shortages catalysing conflicts, which made face-to-face violence and use of *poisin* or sorcery a problem (Mitchell 2000: 199; for a discussion of sorcery and urban violence in Vanuatu, see Banks 1993: 107–109; Eves 2013). Some of the guards had been disenfranchised from land and communities as a result of past poor behaviour, which distanced them from their families, although some of these relationships were said to be possible to redeem. Others said that they had had limited access to customary fraternities, either because as migrants they were away from their clan or ethnic groups or, for locals, because they did not have enough family resources or connections to sponsor initiation into the Dukduk Society (gatherings of the Tolai secret men's society) (Banks 1993). The guards said that children who had been adopted, who were of mixed ethnic parentage, or had divorced parents were more likely to be excluded from initiation.

The company deliberately fostered a pseudo-military workplace environment, with attendant prioritisation of discipline and loyalty. Guards were punished in approximations of codes used in military units or, at least, military units as portrayed in popular action films and television shows (Macintyre 2008; Mitchell 2000). During their working week, guards were expected to salute on the approach of the company owner, either on foot or as his car passed, leaping to their feet, hands clasped at chest height and loudly saying, 'Boss!' Failure to do so resulted in having to drop where they stood and, in the familiar stand-by of Hollywood army movies, do a number of push-ups. Less innocuous forms of discipline were also used. Although the guards were only supposed to work eight-hour shifts, often, they said, their relieving shift would not turn up. But if they left their post before someone else changed with them, or fell asleep while on duty and were caught, this might be cause for a beating from superior officers. Although the guards reported dissatisfaction with many aspects of their work, including the threat of violence from members of the public while on duty, I have no record of them complaining about being physically 'disciplined' in the workplace.

Indeed, the guards talked about using similar kinds of force to keep community peace, particularly in mixed ethnic communities where 'people have got different ways of thinking, different ideology' (Group discussion with Kokopo Security Guards, 12 September 2012). As Lars Buur observes, where violence is disciplinary it 'is nearly always directed at the future in the form of "prevention", "change of behaviour", and "learning the right way"' (2008: 577). One man gave an example of a youth from East Sepik who was branded a ring-leader regarding trouble in the community.

> He's a *bikhet* boy, *bikhet stret*. Like, he drinks a lot and he influences others to be like him; when he goes to Rabaul he goes around with street boys and they all cause trouble. The thing is, when he drinks, he swears. Swears inside the community, tok nogut inside the community. He has no respect for the bigman or the elders inside the community. People hate him for it, for his attitude … But the thing is, whatever you do, you have to face the consequences. So one time, this boy went back home and everyone beat him up. It was big, he was even cut with a knife and got admitted to the *haus sik*. When he came out of the hospital, he'd changed. He was a good boy again (group discussion with Kokopo Security Guards, 19 September 2012).

In this example, the violence used was narrated as having been redemptive and helpful, both for the individual being 'taught a lesson' and the community who gained a reformed citizen.

The guards talked a lot about being 'caught between' the village and town, *kastom* and state laws, saying, '*Ol konfus i stap. Wanen we lo behind?*' (Everyone is confused. Which direction should we follow?) Where are we? Where do we belong?' (group discussion with Kokopo Security Guards 19 September 2012). They felt that they imperfectly straddled ways of supporting themselves and their families, being on the periphery of land access, social support and waged labour (Munro, this volume).

These same dynamics of precarious livelihoods and uncertain social statuses that the guards said they felt also appear often in explanations of contemporary violence and crime in Papua New Guinea. Sinclair Dinnen writes:

> The relationship between the security industry and *raskolism* is essentially symbiotic. Even though private security feeds off high levels of crime and insecurity, criminals looking for legitimate openings have shown consistent preference for employment in the security business …

> The practical skills of *raskolism*, associated with the masculine attributes of toughness and physical prowess, are seen as consistent with those required by security guards. These positions also require few formal qualifications (2001: 97).

At various points in their lives, men might drift in and out of practicing *raskolism* and being part of a mob of 'concerned citizens'; identifying on the one hand as deserving or easy targets of theft or violence, and on the other as *bikhets* in need of discipline. Christine Stewart also identifies that police, security guards and *raskols* exist on a:

> continuum ... [sharing] class origins and ideals of masculine comportment and consumption ... both groups feel betrayed by a state which fails to provide employment for the unemployed (the *raskols*) or decent living and working conditions for those it does employ (the police) (2014: 53).

Violence as an expression of masculinity and as an expression of frustration at the disappointments attendant to late capitalism for many in PNG are shared across different articulations of precarious livelihoods, particularly in urban settings and resource enclaves.

There are few spaces where the boundary between security enforcer and potential *raskol* is more porous than within the security industry itself. Security represents one of the few formal employment opportunities for men with limited qualifications, and access to (and sometimes interest in) agricultural livelihoods (Dinnen 2001). Certainly not every guard has been involved in crime, or vice versa, but many belong to the same demographic of disenfranchised—and disenchanted—young men.

Although crime and violence are threats to wellbeing and condemned by women and men who are potential victims, there is, at the same time, a certain empathy for *raskols* and 'big head' youths in communities. In workshops exploring community perceptions of crime in Lae, a city badly affected by violent crime, Martha Macintyre found that:

> the word 'frustration' (used by Tok Pisin as well as English speakers) was used to describe the emotion that women believed inspired men and adolescent boys to smoke marijuana, drink alcohol and behave violently. This term recurred in workshops with police and was invoked to both explain and excuse illegal violence (2008: 182).

Reinforcing the arguments made here, women participating in the workshops stated that as well as beer, guns and marijuana, *raskols* and police all needed to be got rid of in order to make communities safe, with one participant saying, 'who can tell the difference?' (ibid.). Similarly, Dinnen found that 'much of the discussion of *raskol* crime moves between its essentially passive depiction as a symptom of deepening inequalities, and its significance as a form of political dissent' (2001: 47).

Anti-social behaviour thus takes on meaning as a social stand against feelings of disempowerment and those said to have caused it: government, 'elites', and 'all the people who don't take notice of them' (Macintyre 2008: 182). Dinnen writes:

> Many *raskols* do try to legitimate their activities by reference to government failure to deliver essential services, lack of economic opportunities, social injustice, and growing levels of corruption among the national elite. These views also underlie the ambivalence in popular perceptions of *raskolism* in many parts of the country (2001: 47–48).

Community understanding, however, has its limits. Young men who turn to crime are not, after all, the only ones who must work to navigate precarity and its attendant disappointment and frustration. By reacting with righteous aggression, they add to the difficulties of others in their communities combating the same political economies that impede livelihoods and access to basic services. Keir Martin observes that around Rabaul, East New Britain, 'many Tolai are aware of the economic changes that have led to this state of affairs and therefore have some sympathy with the plight of these young men' (2013: 149). At the same time, the youths are regarded with frustration and embarrassment, their own alleged laziness and poor attitudes placed at fault, meaning that 'most of the time they are cast as the problems themselves' (ibid.: 150).

Macintyre shows how the aggressive masculinity that results in illegal violence is 'simultaneously sociable—for it aims to gain the admiration of other men—and anti-social, in that it is often harmful, illegal and disruptive of social harmony' (2008: 180). Despite the inaccurate connotations of the term 'gangs' when applied to crime in Papua New Guinea,[2] criminal activity is nonetheless distinctly social. It is undertaken as much for prestige and to attain membership of a group in the face of being part of 'a whole generation that the new economy seems to have

---

2   The word 'gang' is used here to describe groups of peers, some of whom engage in criminal activity, but others who do not (Dinnen 2001). The term has a quite different meaning than when associated with gang activity in other parts of the world. Loyalty and affiliation is less fixed, and membership far more mobile than, for example, might be normal for gangs in cities and prisons of the US or South Africa.

cast as being surplus to requirements' (Martin 2013: 152), as for material gain or to vent 'frustration'. The comportment of young men—from their clothes, to their hairstyle, consumption of music and even the ways that they pose in photos, throwing up hand signs borrowed from globalised hip hop and dancehall 'gangsta' style (Alim 2009)—speaks to a Melanesian version of what Macintyre refers to as 'youth polyculture' (2008: 183).

The ways in which men seek to move beyond social acceptance within a peer group, and try to gain respectability and the social acceptance of the whole by proving themselves to be good citizens is, as I have argued, multidirectional. As Joseph, a former security guard, put it to me when discussing his future hopes, he wants 'to be a good human resource for my country' (Interview with Joseph, Kokopo, 16 April 2012). This clearly also highlights the neoliberal contours of such ambitions. Acting as a security guard is a way to apply learned ways of gaining social power as a male through violence, towards new frameworks of personhood; aggressive masculinity for good rather than for ill. Securitisation narratives allow violence to be constructed as punitive rather than retributive, disciplinary instead of vindictive, and therefore as contributing to modern development futures (Buur 2008). In the remainder of this chapter, I turn to a discussion of the different ways this logic was made malleable and utilised in narratives of 'disciplinary' violence by men against women.

Violent meri

Interviewer: What about 'violent woman' in English, how would you say that?

Guard: *Meri bilong pait, bilong kiross, bilong tingting nogut, bilong spak* (Women who fight, who have bad tempers, are suspicious, get drunk) dance at different clubs all the time, go here and there, *pait bilong* man [fight over men] (group discussion with Kokopo Security Guards, 19 September 2012).

The guards insisted that the laws that forbade violence against women were well-known and publicised through community announcements, radio, poster and television campaigns. While still in training, the guards were required to attend workshop sessions about HIV, which included talking about violence in relationships and 'gender roles and responsibilities' (Wardlow 2011). The owner of the company was a vocal supporter of the national and provincial HIV response, and publicly declared his desire to improve the wellbeing, safety and access to rights for local women.

Indeed, Sammy, one of the operations managers I had worked closely with had been fired at the beginning of 2013 because, I was told, the boss had heard that Sammy beat his wife.

The decision of the security firm to fire Sammy because of reports of wife beating was, I thought, laudable. To the best of my knowledge, the first employer in the Province to enforce a similar policy had been PNG Ports, a major sponsor of White Ribbon Day, for whom this was a national policy (PNG Ports Corporation 2013). Making domestic assault a sackable offence made a powerful public statement about the unacceptability of violence against women. And yet, there was incongruity in the fact that the company would damn an act of violence committed by a male staff member against women, when I knew that in normal operations—and in communities—violence was an acceptable means of instilling 'discipline' in men.

In the discussion groups with the guards, it became apparent that there were two ways that this apparent contradiction was reconciled (though these were not mutually exclusive). First, women were talked about as weak, fragile and unable to withstand the kinds of punishment that men could. One guard told me, '*Meri olsem skin bilong em i no strong. Mipla man olsem, skin bilong mipla em strong*' (Women's skin is weak. Us men, our skin is tough) (Group discussion with Kokopo Security Guards, 19 September 2012). Relatedly, hitting women in a household was talked about as a risk to the smooth running of the house.

> '*Nogut yu paitim meri na meri dai lusim yu*' (No good you hit your wife and then she dies and leaves you). Who'll look after the kids? Like, if we were married and I beat you up and broke your ribs, I won't have a woman to cook for me, I'll have to do all the work because you're dead or your hand is broken and so it's hard to wash clothes, things like that (discussion with Silas, North Coast Rabaul, 20 October 2012).

Both arguments, while they did not contradict the admonition to practice non-violence, reinforced inequitable gender stereotypes. The particular focus on prevention of male violence against women becomes justified by a sexist logic that emphasises women's supposed physical weakness, or that they are too useful a tool to damage. This logic undermines the broader aims of anti-violence against women campaigns and of women's equal rights to economic, social and political participation (Merry 2006).

The second line of reasoning determined that violence was only illegitimate if it was unprovoked, excessive and the result of the perpetrator's lack of control or bad temper. In discussion about my research with Silas (an older man who was not a security guard), he noted how welcome it was that police had been doing more awareness raising about the laws related to violence against women in his area. 'You don't see as many women with black eyes and broken arms walking around', he said (discussion with Silas, North Coast Rabaul, 20 October 2012). He had observed that there was less legitimacy in village courts or in informal moots, such as ward counsel mediations, when men claimed that it was their 'right' to hit their wife because of a biblical principle of wifely submission, because they had paid bride price, or because she had pushed him to it; less *pasin sori long ol man* (overt bias favouring men). Silas saw that the law had become stronger, and people had to follow it in the name of development.

He had concerns about the law, however. Silas was unequivocal that it was good that *bikhet* or *humbug man* were more scared of legal consequences and being reported to the police or ward counsellor. They were more likely to think twice about hitting their wives because they had not prepared dinner on time, or they had got home late from work or from the market. However, he asked, what are families supposed to do, what should a husband do, if his wife is going around with other men? What if she is neglecting her children, and her duties, her garden and home to go dancing, drinking beer and sleeping around? If a man hits her to discipline her, then he's breaking the law. If he doesn't, she won't listen to what he says, and the family will break down. People will laugh at him and talk, they won't respect him in the community. What then?

As seen in the quote at the beginning of this section, where I asked the guards to translate the phrase 'a violent woman' into Tok Pisin, feminine violence was defined as behaviour that transgressed conservative imaginings of women's social place as much as outright aggression. 'Big head' women invite violence, push men out of control, and need to be taught lessons by men as the disciplinary heads of households (Banks 2000; Bradley 1992). In these accounts, the guards made distinctions between 'serious' attacks that a *man bilong pait* might enact, and 'just' a slap or a punch done to keep discipline in the household. By creating hierarchies of violence, men were able to minimise the seriousness of their own actions and mitigate their own culpability. As Mo Hume writes, the 'key to men's narratives was that they were not the worst [offenders]' (2009: 82).

In talking about their own and friends' experiences of becoming frustrated and hitting women, the guards oscillated between expressing regret and blame. They were regretful that they did not know how else they could respond to egregious insults or insubordination from women in their households, especially wives and girlfriends, and still maintain pride and respect from peers and family. They experienced blame and anger towards the victim of violence for provoking the assault. Even the courts were complicit in reinforcing this line of thinking. A senior magistrate at Kokopo District Court had informed police officers working with the Family and Sexual Violence Unit (FSVU) that, contrary to National Directions Orders pertaining to Interim Protection Orders (IPOs), he would not be issuing the emergency restraining orders for domestic violence complaints on first hearings. One of the officers told me that the magistrate:

> said that lots of women used to come into the court and get an IPO against their husband, where actually, they were in the wrong, they had provoked the situation that had come up and when their husband hit them, they ran to the police and said that it was all their husband's fault (interview with FSVU, Kokopo, April 2013).

Despite recognising that 'making the action' was illegal and wrong, underlying narratives of 'legitimate' male-on-male discipline in their recounting or reflections on domestic violence meant that acts of vindictiveness or rage could be reframed as disciplinary encounters, where women were 'taught a lesson' (Eves 2006). Equally troubling, this same logic was used to abdicate perpetrator responsibility for sexual assault, including gang rape, or *lainups* (Banks 2000; Hukula 2012; Lepani 2008). Such acts, acknowledged to be driven by *mangal* or selfish desire on the part of the man, were still said to be have been brought about by women being 'money-minded'. If they had not been out at night, or if they had been willing sex partners who had not requested money as compensation for sex, then they would not have been forced. Here too, men could use the complicity of legal institutions to blackmail women into sex, particularly if the perpetrator knew the victim's previous sexual partners.

> If a friend of mine tells me that he's already slept with a woman, I will want to have sex with her too, it's a competition ... [if the woman doesn't want to] I'd force her, because I know the kind of woman she is, she just wants money or drinks. Or, I can threaten her with the law. If she doesn't go with me, then I'll take her to court, because she's already committed adultery (group discussion with Kokopo Security Guards, 3 October 2012).

I argue that all of these acts exist on a continuum where both securitisation and discipline are invoked as explanations for punitive reactions against anyone suspected of causing 'social problems'. This allowed some men to manipulate discourses of securitisation to explain even the most vile acts of rape. Such explanations were not unproblematised by the men who weaved these narratives—punitive rape was not accepted as something that a 'good' man would do. However, for those that tried to rationalise acts of violence against women, the ability to be a good man was contingent on being in the company of good women. Women were positioned as the gatekeepers upholding community morality as well as being the catalyst for moral downfall. Rights-focused campaigns concentrate on gender equity from law and justice and from the health sector and seek to undermine the legitimacy and traction of these arguments. These have not been without success, including the unanimous passing of the *Family Protection Act* by National Parliament in 2013. However, they have not yet destabilised the element of aspirational masculinity, which holds that maintaining family discipline and upholding community discipline are part of being a good man (Howson 2014). The malleability of securitisation and discipline as a way of discursively framing acts of violence, and the paucity of responses from state and community authorities supposed to hold men accountable, mean that *raskol* acts were allowed to be reframed by men to fit with a *raitman* (upright, honorable man) ethos.

Conclusion

In this chapter, I have shown the continuum of how narratives of security and discipline are used to legitimate different forms of violence—from violence against criminals to rationalisations of rape. In doing so, I have explored the connections between historic legacies of male violence in many ethnic groups across Papua New Guinea and the narratives of violence today, the ways that brutal encounters with colonial 'pacification' have shaped attitudes to law and order (Jolly, Stewart with Brewer (eds) 2012), and the rupturing effect of multi-ethnic, neoliberal modernity and change on social selves and social controls in contemporary Papua New Guinea. To this mix, I also add development discourses—those that speak to a need to avoid state fragility and market-oriented definitions of 'insecurity', and those that seek to address violence against women by men as a distinct category of violence. The combined histories and continuing efforts to navigate precarity are used in various ways to excuse, explain and attempt to construct solutions. Inevitably, the approaches of different perspectives and actors within this milieu must be negotiated and reframed. All of these negotiations occur as part of existing power dynamics and struggles; all of them are, indelibly and critically, gendered. Hume reminds us that 'all research on violence is informed by silences … restricting knowledge about violence and actively undermining efforts to challenge it'. Further:

> as long as men and masculinities remain ignored in most analyses of violence, our knowledge remains limited, and normative understandings of violence that fail to uncritically unpack and problematize its masculinised dimensions are privileged (2009: 78).

My contention in this chapter is that ignoring the broader application of aggressive masculinity manifest in securitisation narratives, the benefits that such behaviours provide to bearers, and the harm violence causes men as well as women, limits the efficacy of interventions against violence.

References

Akmeemana, Sakuntala, Reno Diwa, Nicholas Menzies and Laura Bailey. 2014. *Crimes and Disputes*. Research and Dialogue Series. Washington: World Bank.

Alim, H. Samy. 2009. 'Straight outta Compton, straight aus München: Global linguistic flows, identities, and the politics of language in a global hip hop nation'. In *Global Linguistic Flows: Hip Hop Cultures, Youth Identities, and the Politics of Language*, ed. H. Samy Alim, Awad Ibrahim and Alastair Pennycook, pp. 1–24. New York: Routledge.

Amnesty International. 2006. *Papua New Guinea: Violence Against Women: Not Inevitable, Never Acceptable*. Port Moresby: Amnesty International.

Anderson, Stephanie. 2016. 'Manus Island detention centre to be shut, Papua New Guinea Prime Minister Peter O'Neill says'. *ABC News*, 27 April. Online: www.abc.net.au/news/2016-04-27/png-pm-oneill-to-shut-manus-island-detention-centre/7364414 (accessed 26 June 2016).

Banks, Cyndi. 2000. 'Contextualising sexual violence: Rape and carnal knowledge in Papua New Guinea'. In *Reflections on Violence in Melanesia*, ed. Sinclair Dinnen and Allison Ley, pp. 83–104. Leichhardt and Canberra: Hawkins Press and Asia Pacific Press.

——. 1993. *Women in Transition: Social Control in Papua New Guinea*. Canberra: Australian Institute of Criminology.

Bradley, Christine. 1992. *Final Report on Domestic Violence* 14. Port Moresby: Papua New Guinea Law Reform Commission.

Buur, Lars. 2008. 'Democracy and its discontents: Vigilantism, sovereignty and human rights in south Africa'. *Review of African Political Economy* 35(118): 571–84. doi.org/10.1080/03056240802569250.

Callinan, Rory. 2013. 'Australia funds lethal brute squad'. *Age*, 4 August. Online: www.theage.com.au/victoria/australia-funds-lethal-brute-squad-20130803-2r6g1.html (accessed 10 August 2014).

Consultative Implementation and Monitoring Council (CIMC) and Family and Sexual Violence Action Committee (FSVAC). n.d. *Wife Beating is a Crime*. Port Moresby: Family and Sexual Violence Action Committee.

Davey, Melissa. 2014. 'Manus security firm, G4S, responsible for February violence, says law centre'. *Guardian*, 23 September. Online: www.theguardian.com/world/2014/sep/23/manus-security-firm-g4s-responsible-for-february-violence-says-law-centre (accessed 15 April 2015).

Dinnen, Sinclair. 2001. *Law and Order in a Weak State: Crime and Politics in Papua New Guinea*. Honolulu: University of Hawai'i Press.

Dinnen, Sinclair and Abby Mcleod. 2008. 'The quest for integration: Australian approaches to security and development in the Pacific Islands'. *Security Challenges* 4(2): 23–43.

Eves, Richard. 2013. 'Sorcery and Witchcraft in Papua New Guinea: Problems in Definition'. State, Society and Governance in Melanesia, in brief 2013/12. Canberra: The Australian National University.

———. 2006. *Exploring the Role of Men and Masculinities in Papua New Guinea in the 21st Century: How to Address Violence in Ways that Generate Empowerment for Both Men and Women.* Report for Caritas Australia. Online: xyonline.net/sites/default/files/Eves,%20Exploring%20role% 20of%20men%20PNG.pdf (accessed 17 November 2016).

Goldstein, Daniel M. 2010. 'Toward a critical anthropology of security'. *Current Anthropology* 51(4): 487–517. doi.org/10.1086/655393.

Independent State of Papua New Guinea. 2004. *Security (Protection) Industry Act.* Port Moresby.

Howson, Richard. 2014. 'Re-thinking aspiration and hegemonic masculinity in transnational context'. *Masculinities and Social Change* 3(1): 18–35.

Hukula, Fiona. 2012. 'Conversations with convicted rapists'. In *Engendering Violence in Papua New Guinea*, ed. Margaret Jolly, Christine Stewart with Carolyn Brewer, pp. 197–212. Canberra: ANU E Press. Online: press.anu.edu.au/publications/engendering-violence-papua-new-guinea (accessed 23 August 2016).

Human Rights Watch. 2015. *World Report 2015 Events of 2014.* Human Rights Watch.

———. 2005. *Making Their Own Rules: Police Beatings, Rape, and Torture of Children in PNG.* New York: Human Rights Watch.

Hume, Mo. 2009. 'Researching the gendered silences of violence in El Salvador'. *IDS Bulletin* 40(3): 78–85. doi.org/10.1111/j.1759-5436.2009.00042.x.

Jolly, Margaret, Christine Stewart with Carolyn Brewer (eds). 2012. *Engendering Violence in Papua New Guinea.* Canberra: ANU E Press. Online: press.anu.edu.au/publications/engendering-violence-papua-new-guinea (accessed 23 August 2016).

Klugman, Jeni, Lucia Hanmer, Sarah Twigg, Tazeen Hasan, Jennifer McCleary-Sills and Julieth Santamaria. 2014. *Voice and Agency: Empowering Women and Girls for Shared Prosperity.* Washington: World Bank. doi.org/10.1596/978-1-4648-0359-8.

Lakhani, Sadaf and Alys M. Willman. 2014. *Gates, Hired Guns and Mistrust: Business Unusual: The Cost of Crime and Violence to Businesses in PNG.* Washington DC: World Bank Group.

Lepani, Katherine. 2008. 'Mobility, violence and the gendering of HIV in Papua New Guinea'. *The Australian Journal of Anthropology* 19(2): 150–64. doi.org/10.1111/j.1835-9310.2008.tb00119.x.

Macintyre, Martha. 2012. 'Gender violence in Melanesia and the problem of Millennium Development Goal No. 3'. In *Engendering Violence in Papua New Guinea*, ed. Margaret Jolly, Christine Stewart with Carolyn Brewer, pp. 239–66. Canberra: ANU E Press. Online: press.anu.edu.au/publications/engendering-violence-papua-new-guinea (accessed 23 August 2016).

———. 2008. 'Police and thieves, gunmen and drunks: Problems with men and problems with society in Papua New Guinea'. *The Australian Journal of Anthropology* 19(2): 179–93. doi.org/10.1111/j.1835-9310.2008.tb00121.x.

Martin, Keir. 2013. *The Death of the Big Men and the Rise of the Big Shots: Custom and Conflict in East New Britain.* New York and Oxford: Berghan Books.

Mcleod, Abby and Martha Macintyre. 2010. 'The Royal Papua New Guinea constabulary'. In *Civic Insecurity: Law, Order and HIV in Papua New Guinea*, ed. Vicki Luker and Sinclair Dinnen, pp. 167–78. Canberra: ANU E Press. Online: press.anu.edu.au/publications/series/state-society-and-governance-melanesia/civic-insecurity (accessed 23 August 2016).

McVeigh, Karen. 2015. 'Canada mining firm compensates Papua New Guinea woman after alleged rapes'. *Guardian Online*, 4 April. Online: www.theguardian.com/world/2015/apr/03/canada-barrick-gold-mining-compensates-papua-new-guinea-women-rape (accessed 15 April 2015).

Merry, Sally Engle. 2006. *Human Rights and Gender Violence: Translating International Law into Local Justice.* Chicago: University of Chicago Press.

Mitchell, Jean. 2000. 'Violence as continuity: violence as rupture—narratives from an urban settlement in Vanuatu'. In *Reflections on Violence in Melanesia*, ed. Sinclair Dinnen and Allison Ley, pp. 189–208. Leichhardt and Canberra: Hawkins Press and Asia Pacific Press.

O'Connor, Tim, Sharni Chan and James Goodman. 2006. 'Australian aid: Promoting insecurity?' In *The Reality of Aid Report 2006*, ed. The Reality of Aid, pp. 175–89. Quezon City: The Reality of Aid.

Pacific Economic Monitor. 2014. 'Papua New Guinea Economic and Labor Market Update'. July 2014. In *Economic Update*. Philippines: Asian Development Bank.

Papua New Guinea–Australia Law and Justice Partnership. 2013. 'Fact Sheet 9: Royal Papua New Guinea Constabulary (RPNGC)'. Canberra: Papua New Guinea–Australia Law and Justice Partnership.

PNG Ports Corporation. 2013. 'PNGPCL support "Haus Krai" on gender violence,' 21 May. Online: www.pngports.com.pg/index.php/latest-news/1233-pngpcl-support-haus-krai-on-gender-violence (accessed 20 April 2015).

Scott, Ben. 2005. *Re-imagining PNG: Culture, Democracy and Australia's Role*. Lowy Institute Paper No. 09. Double Bay: Lowy Institute for International Policy.

Security Industries Authority (SIA). 2014. 'Current status of the security business in PNG,' Security Companies Information. *Security Industries Authority*. Online: sia.gov.pg/seccomps.html (accessed 20 August 2014).

Stewart, Christine. 2014. *Name, Shame and Blame: Criminalising Consensual Sex in Papua New Guinea*. Canberra: ANU Press. Online: press.anu.edu.au/publications/name-shame-and-blame (accessed 23 August 2016).

Wardlow, Holly. 2011. 'The task of the HIV translator: Transforming global AIDS knowledge in an awareness workshop'. *Medical Anthropology: Cross-Cultural Studies in Health and Illness* 31(5): 404–19. doi.org/10.1080/01459740.2012.661002.

Wolfe, Asher. 2014. 'Manus Island guards unlicensed, says PNG regulator'. *SBS News* Australia, 17 March. Online: www.sbs.com.au/news/article/2014/03/17/manus-island-guards-unlicensed-says-png-regulator (accessed 10 August 2014).

2

Gender struggles of educated men in the Papuan highlands

Jenny Munro
The Australian National University

Men are often said to resist, or even lash out against, changing gender norms where they seem likely to advantage women and displace their own authority. As Martha Macintyre succinctly puts it, 'For women to gain the control over their own lives and bodies that "eliminating violence" entails, men are going to have to lose it' (2012: 239). Scholarship that foregrounds men's perspectives and lived engagements with contemporary gender values and expectations can contribute nuanced insights into gendered struggles around inequality and cultural change (e.g. Brison 1995; Kempf 2002; Taylor 2008). Drawing on periods of ethnographic research with educated Dani men from the Papuan highlands (Indonesia) between 2005 and 2013, in this chapter I consider what insights can be generated by looking at the experiences and views of men who actively consider and try to pursue modern gender ideals, but whose efforts may be thwarted, go awry, or result in unpredictable outcomes. I conclude that innovative gender ideas are not always translated into practice, and practicing equality in gender relations may be challenged by broader conditions that make unequal relations the path of least resistance. We can improve our understanding of persisting gender inequalities by examining men's struggles with gender values and by asking how gender equalities may be thwarted before they gain traction.

Situating indigenous masculinities in highlands Papua

Papuan masculinities are shaped by competing ideals, challenges, and structural constraints, and are uniquely positioned as Melanesian, Indonesian and indigenous. What Margaret Jolly writes is true for Papua: 'Indigenous masculinities have been formed in relation to, as much as resistance against, hegemonic foreign models; and through such histories, hybrid hegemonies have emerged' (2008: 3). Martin Slama and Jenny Munro (2015) describe the lived space of Papuans as flush with tensions generated by Indonesian views that relegate Papuans to the 'stone-age' (and may wish them to remain there), and 'real-time' practices and conditions in an era of new connections, mobilities and technologies. The notion of being 'left behind' permeates gender as well as ethnic and cultural constructions in Indonesia (Elmhirst 2007), and has been for many decades a claim by which the state advances its power, attempting to displace local forms of authority, understandings and lifeways with 'modern' national ones (Li 1999).

Views from Papua New Guinea, on the other side of the island, describe masculinities in crisis (Knauft 2011) and new articulations of male identity through monetary prowess, commodity consumption, sexual practices and Christian values (Bainton 2008; Cox and Macintyre 2014; Martin 2013). In Papua, the biggest ideological threats to indigenous masculinities are the discourses that relegate cultural practices and values to the tribal past and position culture and black racial heritage as something to be ashamed of (Munro 2015; Stasch 2015). While Papua's frontier economy is burgeoning, it is not controlled by Papuans, and Papuan men are not necessarily the main players in it (Kirksey 2012). Unlike Papua New Guinea, Papuans compete with Indonesians for urban jobs, and are a minority in most urban centres and both provincial capitals. Masculine difference, rather than being constructed primarily around class distinctions, is racialised.

In Indonesia, former dictator Suharto's 'New Order' policies governing civil life until 1998 were emphatically gendered (Robinson 2000: 141). Smoothing out regional and cultural gender variations in this vast archipelago was part of a nationalising process. Pam Nilan suggests that 'since the end of the New Order in 1998, matters of cultural leadership on gender issues have become more complicated' (2009: 330). Indonesian masculinities now evoke:

> various kinds of pressure: to become a good citizen and dependable provider for the family on the one hand, and on the other hand, to match the fantasy images of global 'hypermasculinity'—tough, hard and heroic (ibid.: 327).

Pressures of citizenship and provider, as well as toughness and heroicism, provoke questions of a different character in Papua, where citizenship is more highly contested, at times denied by the state and its security agents, sometimes rejected outright by Papuans who dispute the conditions of their entry into Indonesia in 1963 and the violence and inequality that has been delivered by authorities over the past six decades (see Hernawan 2015). The sort of toughness that might be welcomed on Java is decidedly less welcome among Papuan men, at least from the perspective of government and military personnel trying to silence critiques of the state.

Even if the state's hegemonic efforts to define gender roles have waned, ideologies and practices of development and modernisation continue to shape gender practices, from the domain of everyday life to the interventions devised to change gender inequalities. Although the space of development in Papua so far does not reflect the same focus on, or public messaging about, men that occurs in Papua New Guinea (Lusby 2014 and this volume), for example, there is a similar tendency among development actors to see gender in oversimplified terms for the sake of program implementation. Feryana Wakerkwa (2015) records failed development and government programs in the highlands and other locales in Papua that have tried to unilaterally rectify women's poverty, lack of rights, or disempowerment without involving men in discussions about gender roles, norms or broader power asymmetries.

Nilan (2009) and others argue that the 'Father' (*Bapak*) masculinity of the Suharto era, in which the *bapak* held authority over the family, the village and the state in the name of national development, has waned and become more complex over the past decade. In Indonesia more broadly, recent trends and shifts have been influential for gender relations. However, patterns of urbanisation, later age of marriage, fertility control and the rise in women's labour force participation (Jones 2005) cannot be presumed to be occurring in Papua, nor can we surmise that these trends might be having the same impact as they are said to be having in the rest of Indonesia. The *bapak* persona perhaps continues to have a stronger hold in Papua than the rest of Indonesia. In Papua today, *bapak* is most likely an indigenous man, perhaps the governor or a district head who provides for an entourage of supporters, or perhaps an entrepreneur who commands and controls the livelihoods of a barrage of poor male labourers. He might be a church leader whose commitments promote religious as well as development-related interests among his congregation. *Bapak* is not unrivalled, as he still competes with Indonesians and the central government for his role in local development (Bertrand 2014; Chauvel 2011).

In Papua as elsewhere it is not only the state, but religious influences as well, that generate particular challenges, tensions and directions for what it means to be a modern man. In Indonesia, religious piety is widely promoted as a modern attribute, and adhering to a world religion is a necessary facet of citizenship, though conservative religious views inscribe gender hierarchies in marriage and family life more generally. Through religion Papuans are connected to other global moderns, and in theory religions promote claims to equality that may otherwise be difficult to come by in Papua (Slama 2015; Timmer 2015).

The Baliem Valley

The Baliem Valley of the central highlands is the traditional territory of the Dani. Traditionally, Dani men achieved political and social standing by building alliances and redistributing wealth at large-scale ceremonial exchanges of pigs, especially for bride price, which in turn depended on (and generated) wives to create gardens and descendants. Big men achieved standing based on their ability to do good things for others, providing leadership through words, actions and networks (Alua 2006). Women and men engaged in distinct roles and activities, and occupied separate social and physical spaces.

The first permanent presence of foreigners in the valley, namely Catholic and Protestant missionaries who established posts in Wamena in 1954, set in motion new trajectories for gender roles, relations and identities. Male activities were of particular interest to missionaries. Some big men fought against missionaries and protested their agendas, while others sought to draw new authority from affiliations with them (Farhadian 2001, 2003; Naylor 1974). Boys and young men were engaged as religious pupils and school students. In the 1960s, the offer of an educational migration to school outside the valley, or being engaged as an indigenous Bible teacher, were some of the first opportunities for a lifestyle not primarily characterised by subsistence horticulture. Particular men's activities and roles were banned or at least discouraged by missionaries, including many forms of exchange, polygamy and tribal war. A 1977 war in the Baliem Valley saw Indonesian troops attacking villages to dispel resistance among those who rejected Indonesian rule, in the name of pacifying tribal warfare. Dani men were overwhelmingly seen as 'primitives' in need of the state's development interventions. Highland men's traditional attire, the penis-sheath (*koteka* in Indonesian or *holim* in Dani), symbolised this need for authorities and Indonesian and other onlookers. The first official Indonesian government development intervention in the highlands, Operation Koteka, was named after it.

The city of Wamena, now home to about 40,000 inhabitants, half of whom are indigenous (mainly locals) and half of whom are non-indigenous Indonesian migrants, has emerged as an economic and political hub for the populous, rugged central highlands, despite being accessible only by air. Especially in the city and on its fringes, subsistence horticulture has been abandoned or partially redirected towards a market economy, and indeed many inhabitants around the town are now city dwellers who do not garden at all. Indonesians dominate the commercial sector as shopkeepers and investors and, despite some shifts in hiring patterns, maintain an important presence in government roles. Indonesians also dominate the security sector, which maintains an active presence in the everyday lives of local inhabitants.

Wamena is situated in the oldest administrative district (*kabupaten*) in the Jayawijaya highlands and, as such, patterns of development, employment and government services differ from the new districts emerging in remote areas. However, Jayawijaya has seen a proliferation of sub-districts, each with an appointed local indigenous inhabitant as subdistrict head. Some employment for indigenous locals has been generated in the bureaucracies of these subdistricts. Employment in road construction or driving trucks are examples of ways that mainly indigenous men engage in 'development' around the district; Dani men express frustration when labour jobs are taken by Indonesians whom they view as physically inferior (Munro and Wetipo 2013; Munro 2015). Wamena attracts many indigenous highlanders to its urban vibe, better functioning services and, usually, improved safety and security relative to remote posts and villages where security forces monitor civilians and fight 'separatists' with destructive consequences for local inhabitants.

There are significant tensions between how educated highlands men see themselves and how they are often regarded and treated by Indonesians and, to a lesser extent, coastal Papuans (Munro 2015). Part of this tension arises from the potent ideologies, and overrated promises, of the transformative power of education, which encourage educated men and women to aspire to social status, prestige and respect by virtue of their achievements in spite of potent racism and other structural kinds of oppression. Papuans also regard education as an achievement that confers some superiority, an obligation to do good for others and to contribute to development, as well as a resource that enables resistance. While in Indonesia education has been intended to nationalise and 'homogenise' as much as 'develop' the populace, in Papua (and in other 'remote' areas) education has enveloped a more explicit civilising mission that is now an integral part of Papuans' own understandings of their place in society and options for advancement (see Stasch 2015).

The following case study explores the life of a Dani man I have known since 2005, positioning Yohannes's experiences in the context of his town and neighbourhood, his family and marriage, work and church activities. Rather than normalcy marked by crisis, or continuity marred by disruption, his story demonstrates a persistent struggle to position himself as 'modern', and to enact incipient ideas about gender equality, in spite of constant insecurity and instability.

Yohannes

Yohannes (not his real name) is a public servant in Wamena. Aged in his 40s, he is of the first generation of highlanders to complete an Indonesian education from start to finish. Yohannes's education was also a Catholic education; the school was run by Dutch priests as well as teachers from eastern parts of Indonesia. Although his family has land near the Baliem River, Yohannes lives with his wife and two children in the original part of Wamena city referred to as Misi after the Catholic mission.

A bustling market area has grown along the main street near Yohannes's house, along with an orphanage and some motorbike repair shops. The Indonesian-owned and operated shops (*kios*) line the sides of the street while dirt areas in front are occupied by Dani women selling vegetables and fruit. Some shops are now home to game consoles like PlayStation where kids can play for a fee; similarly, Yohannes can charge his mobile phone at a *kios* if the power is out at home. His neighbourhood was largely destroyed in October 2000 during the worst documented inter-ethnic violence that has ever happened in Papua. The violence broke out when police and other security forces attacked various locations where the Papuan independence flag was raised, killing one person, shooting 10 others, and beating and arresting dozens (Mote and Rutherford 2001). At least 24 migrants and seven Papuans were killed in the melee. Since the incident, a new military command unit has set up near the market. Misi remains one of the most volatile parts of town—a dangerous mix of soldiers, police, new and long-time migrants, and indigenous inhabitants from all over the central highlands, including street youth and those who sniff glue (*anak aibon*). Fights break out, people are treated violently by police or soldiers, and hungry local inhabitants pace through the overstuffed shops.

From Yohannes's house it is a short walk to the We River, a relatively shallow, turbulent, wide river that drains from the peaks of the snowy Puncak Mountains. In contrast to the multi-ethnic town, across the river are the traditional homes and gardens of Dani and other central highlanders who have moved to the area.

Yohannes first applied for a job in the public service in 2000 when he had only a high school degree. At the time, this should not have been a problem, but when I first met him he had already been trying unsuccessfully for about five years. Then, through what he described as a 'miraculous' series of events, one day in 2008 Yohannes read his name in a list of successful public service entrants published in the provincial newspaper. Despite being happy to be employed, a 'blessing' that he saw as a result of his efforts to be a better Christian, he expressed mixed feelings about his work. While it was essential for earning money he also described it as participating in a state that he does not believe in, and working for a country that does not respect his people and does not consider them worthy of an equal role in their own land. He regrets having to put on a civil servant uniform, which 'makes me feel like I'm in school again' (Wamena, 7 June 2009), but appreciates that unlike many civil servants he actually has work to do at the office, which helps pass the time.

Yohannes's wife, Celestina (not her real name), is an educated woman from his cultural group. He did not pay bride price, unusual at the time, because her father said Celestina was smart and he wanted her to finish her schooling and live in the city. Celestina was emotional when she told me about this wish, expressing how fortunate she and Yohannes felt that this was her father's wish for her future. Very progressive, they thought, for a big man with three wives. Yohannes said:

> I really felt that responsibility. He was being very generous, and he wanted me to save money for our future and I told him that the main thing, the important thing is that we were going to live in town and Celestina would have a better life and make use of her education (Wamena, 7 June 2009).

Yohannes supported Celestina, and when she finished high school they moved in together. Despite Celestina being the first young woman to graduate from high school from her village (over the bridge), she was not able to get work either, until 2011. Yohannes does not work in a garden, though Celestina divides her time between her garden over the bridge and her public service job. There is a shop near their house where they are in debt from a decade of purchasing rice, noodles, oil and cigarettes on credit while waiting for cash income to materialise.

Yohannes has, over the years, taken more leadership roles in his church, a small parish over the bridge where one of the local men usually leads the service, except for once a month when a Dutch priest comes over to lead mass, conduct baptisms, etc. In particular, he leads the church's youth group as a mentor. This involves leading discussion groups that talk over particular issues with young people, such as marriage, fights and violence, and how to live a more Christian life. Yohannes has financial expectations and time commitments as well, ranging from contributing to all of the community feasts to organising weekly mass and/or youth group activities.

At least since he joined the public service, Yohannes has struggled with alcohol abuse and with violent behaviour during drinking sessions. He started to really drink, he recalls, when colleagues at work invited him to drink with them, and they would hang out after work especially on or after payday, finishing a couple of bottles of whisky (illegal in Wamena). In 2009 he spoke about how he had 'let go' (*lepas*) of alcohol in conjunction with taking more prominent roles in church and renewing his commitments to being a good Christian. During this time, he focused on mentoring youth, including talking to young men about his experiences with alcohol, such as the time he broke all the windows in his house, or the rather common occasions where he fought with Celestina, shouting abuse or hitting her. He told me he thanked God that he hadn't done more damage or injury, and felt fortunate that his wife and children were still there with him.

In 2009, his wife was finally able to get a job in the public service and they both had renewed hopes that they might be able to improve their lives, or at least their house. Their house had always been a sore point—made of thatched panels, it was falling apart around them, and did little to keep out the cold night air. The roof had fallen in on what was used as a cooking area at the back of the house, so they had gone back to using a fire pit for cooking outdoors. By 2009 there was electricity in the house, but prior to this the children had been reading their school books by candlelight in the evening. With Yohannes receiving half his pay in rice, and the children enrolled at the Catholic school, which charged more fees, there was not enough money, even though Celestina supplied some sweet potatoes and greens from her garden. The family also had some relatives staying with them, at one point a family of four in addition to their other relatives, while the father was away working. They also took on caring for Celestina's sister's daughter Nelly so she could live closer to school. Celestina started work, but as a street cleaner who earned almost no money for her first year of work. During this time, Yohannes also embarked on a university degree program as it was apparent that his high school certificate was not going to be enough for him to keep his job.

During these years there was also some conflict between Celestina and Yohannes over having more children. Yohannes had found himself, in his 40s, wanting more children and since Celestina had not become pregnant he said he suspected it was because either she was secretly using birth control or she had used it at some point in the past and it had rendered her infertile. Celestina, always outspoken, questioned the logic of having more children given their precarious economic situation. It was her recollection that they had agreed about this at some point, though Yohannes seemed to have forgotten their agreement.

In 2013, Yohannes gave Celestina's relative Martin part of their yard and Martin proceeded to build an expensive modern house. It was the sort of house that Yohannes and Celestina had talked about for years. Martin had been working for the provincial government's village development program and through his role in managing and distributing funds had been able to pocket the sort of capital needed to build a good-quality house in Wamena, where the cost of air freight makes everything highly expensive. Shortly thereafter I visited and was surprised to hear that Celestina had left home. Yohannes had been drinking again and had hit Celestina in the face and again damaged the windows in his house. The children, now aged 10 and 13, were still living with their father.

There was discussion among the relatives about whether Celestina wanted some sort of compensation to be paid by Yohannes. After a few weeks, they 'resolved the problem' (*selesaikan masalah*) to use the local phrasing, and Celestina was back home again.

Yohannes's experiences raise a number of themes showing the germination of different gender ideas and practices around bride price, violence, fertility decisions, and female education and employment. A longitudinal view on his life over the span of a decade challenges us to think about violence and alcohol not as problems of uneducated, 'backward' men, but also of educated, progressive men who do not necessarily hold views of women as being 'property', fundamentally inferior, or in need of control by men. In Yohannes's case there were factors to do with other men and their achievements and activities that shaped his struggles with alcohol and violence. His public servant colleagues, both Indonesian and Dani, engaged in binge drinking as an after-hours pastime. His wife's relative, Martin, acquired a lucrative position in the village development program despite having no greater educational attainment than Yohannes. This man was able to build the house that Yohannes and Celestina had been yearning for, right on the land that Yohannes had given to him. It was Martin's wife and three children that Yohannes and Celestina had supported in their home while Martin was away working in other districts.

Relatively early in their marriage, according to Celestina at least, they had decided that they would be more likely to prosper if they limited themselves to having two children, which mirrors the state's promotional messages around birth control. But with the children growing up and very little improvement in their standard of living, Yohannes seemed to be questioning their chosen path of sacrificing the bigger family of typical village life for a small family that could live better in town. It was another massive source of stress for Yohannes that Nelly, the daughter of his wife's sister whom he had raised and put through school, had suddenly turned up pregnant in her first year of high school, perhaps disrupting his notions of female education and men's possible role in supporting it. Family support, influences and pressures play an important role in shaping men's views and actions, as they do in shaping women's and men's expectations of education, employment and marriage (see Spark, this volume).

Yohannes's experiences might give us pause when positioning men as universally resistant to change, or primarily reticent about gender equality and waning authority, though his story is not intended to represent the experiences or views of educated highlands men more broadly. Yohannes does not hold particularly strong views against gender equality, nor does he view hitting his wife as appropriate. He does not subscribe to ideas of wife 'ownership' that accompany the commoditisation of bride price (Wardlow 2006). Yet under the influence of alcohol and stress he is still liable to hurt his wife and create chaos in his family home. It is not necessarily that his masculinity is in crisis, and he lashes out, but rather that the constant structural violence injustice and disruption around him challenges his hold on, and ability to act on, modern gender ideals.

In the remainder of the chapter, I examine particular themes from Yohannes's story, specifically marriage and fertility, stigma and 'security' conditions, drawing in comparisons and contrasts with the gender aspirations and practices of other educated men.

Marriage and fertility

The choice of a spouse, once typically orchestrated by older clan men to build exchange relationships and expand their influence, is an emerging domain in which educated highlands men may try to demonstrate their commitment to modern practices (see Spark, this volume), but in which they are clearly tested by powerful ideas about the beauty, fertility and docility of a young Dani wife. Yohannes was interested in having an educated wife, and a minority of young men in my research have also shared this view. These informants pointed to the economic benefits of having a spouse who would work, probably in the public service, and earn an income, enhancing the couple's position in the 'modern' economy and in town amongst Indonesians. Some men had been raised with the idea that a relatively egalitarian marital partnership (if not necessarily gender equality) is a modern *and* Christian practice, and that men can demonstrate their own modernity by supporting female education (Cox, this volume; Spark, this volume).

A Protestant university student from Wolo, west of Wamena, referring to friends of his who got pregnant while studying in North Sulawesi, a province of eastern Indonesia, pointed out that in his village, the issue of violence would be considered by relatives before allowing a marriage to go ahead:

Even if you wait until you are going to finish [university], like Etinus and Ina, well they are still in big trouble back in the village. Because if you go home like that, about to give birth, you can't get married in church and you have to go to the village and talk with every one, all the elders and the family, it's really difficult. They have to decide whether Etinus is good enough, has he ever hit Ina (Jhon, Tondano (North Sulawesi), 3 April 2006).

The possibility of a marital partnership with an educated woman that existed among university students (both male and female) was in tension with the usual practice of marriage in the Baliem Valley in which men prefer a young wife, in line with traditional norms. In and around Wamena, in many cases, men in the age range of 20–40 years, continue to seek out young women (aged 13–18) whom they consider sexually attractive, and if a pregnancy eventuates, the relationship might be formalised into a marriage (see Butt and Munro 2007 for contrasting cases). Young women (around the age of junior high school) spoke of viewing returnee or visiting male university students as attractive partners who actively pursued them, despite what male university students also said about wanting an educated wife.

A longitudinal view of these relationships also reveals that some husbands became more interested in their young wives having more education and employment opportunities over time, especially after she has already given birth to some children. It seems increasingly common for relatives to demand that a young woman should be allowed and supported to continue her education, not just because the family has paid her school fees and gone without her labour in other domains so that she might contribute financially to the family later in life. In extreme cases an irate father has been known to demand that the man who interrupted his daughter's schooling by impregnating her before marriage repay the cost of her school fees.

Fertility is another dimension of educated masculinities that places men at the centre of competing tensions, desires and expectations. Reproduction has emerged as a crucial domain for political questions concerning who should control and define reproductive practices, and how Papuans can respond to becoming marginalised in relation to large numbers of Indonesian migrants (Butt 2005). Producing children is very important to men and women, though, like Yohannes and Celestina, highlanders and other Papuans face strong pressures from various sources to have fewer children, and less frequently, for the sake of improving family prosperity and maternal health (Munro 2014). Educated town-dwellers experience this pressure more intensely, and having fewer children (and in the 'right' circumstances) is a palpable way to demonstrate one's commitment to modernity and development (Butt 2005; Butt and Munro 2007). But mobility is an increasingly salient component of education. Being away from home offers up new opportunities for sex, partner choice, and childbearing away, to a certain extent, from the surveillance of kin. Male and female university students have suggested that producing the next generation is of equal importance to higher educational achievements. Mobility, education and parenthood are valued markers of modern adulthood, in spite of concerns about sin and breaking cultural rules about premarital pregnancy (Munro 2012). Dani men attending university away from home were very concerned about the consequences of getting a female student pregnant, though they also enjoyed the pursuit of a partner and gained some self-confidence from out-vying other men for the attention of a woman. As Laurence, a university student living in North Sulawesi said:

> My relatives [*kakak-kakak,* literally older siblings] here do not let me get together with girls; I am not allowed to do it. They watch me all the time. I also do not want to destroy someone's daughter, destroy her education. This is not good. If people get married, they usually get pregnant before long. Parents can be very angry if she does this because they want her to study, to graduate, and to return to Wamena and work in an office. They want her to marry someone with status who can be employed … if a woman gets pregnant here in Sulawesi, her parents might order her to go home, but other people actually they just let it be. What can they do if she does not want to listen to them. They hope that the man has status and they hope she can finish even if she has married (16 November 2005).

Young men are clearly aware that young women who are studying at university are expected to graduate and obtain formal employment (see Spark, this volume). Still, most men and women expressed that during migration (*rantau*), abstinence was not realistic nor was it the norm. Because Dani men studying in North Sulawesi vastly outnumbered Dani women, and competed for their attention, many men never found this view tested.

At the same time, birth control and sexual health services were not available to them as unmarried youth (except condoms that could be purchased from some pharmacies). Whether or not young men and women would visit health services and use birth control if it were available raises a host of complex considerations (see Munro 2012, 2014; Butt 2001). One point to make, however, is that even if educated men wished to show commitment to 'modern' ways of relating to women concerning marriage and pregnancy, doing so required working against prevailing conditions and broader norms that make it easier than ever before to have sex outside marriage and get a woman pregnant; to pick up junior high school students from their dorms or homestays and to be in multiple relationships at the same time, while being unable to access birth control. Men may or may not protest particular ideas of gender in marriage and family formation, but they might follow the path of least resistance. Even within the controversial and culturally laden topics of marriage and pregnancy we can see desires, not untested, for innovations in gender relations and practices. Were health services appropriate and accessible, were good-quality educational facilities available closer to home, were desirable jobs more available, might these fledgling ideas and commitments to different articulations of gender and sexuality find space to grow?

Racial stigma and 'security'

Where Yohannes's story highlights stress, not just related to educational expectations, hopes for progress, and structural conditions, other men's experiences more strongly highlight racism, exclusion and violence in shaping educated masculinities and values vis-à-vis women. Avoiding stigma is of particular concern. For example:

> Us Papuans are stigmatised as drunks, especially highlanders. The media is always exaggerating stories of us—we like to drink, we like to get drunk, we like to kill each other. Sometimes what is just a family dispute is presented on TV as a tribal war … So everyone on the outside thinks Papuans are like this … that's just how things are nowadays (Daniel, student/NGO worker, Wamena, 18 June 2012; Munro and Wetipo 2013: 24).

How highlands Papuan men are seen by others is a concern of young, educated men that brings together a cultural emphasis on reputation, surveillance and observation as salient aspects of sociality. It also involves the state of being watched and judged, not only by Indonesians in Wamena, but also by Indonesians who consume news and travel programming on television, Facebook or other internet platforms (Munro 2015: 188).

Educated men and women from the highlands are among the most ardent and active critics of Indonesian rule in Papua. Papuan men (and less so, women) take up active public roles on issues ranging from human rights abuses to women's economic empowerment, on particular policy decisions as well as electoral politics. Although women's participation is typically welcomed, activism is an integral part of how educated men demonstrate 'modern', primarily male-dominated forms of peer leadership while connecting themselves to a broader masculine community. The term 'comrade' (*kawan*) is a popular way for men to address one another that situates men as always and already part of a political movement/community, even when used in everyday speech as a term of endearment. Men of Yohannes's age are leading figures in various movements; some of these men have been jailed for political activism by the Indonesian government. Treating educated Papuan male activists in a demeaning fashion, such as in November 2011 when participants in the 3rd Papuan Congress were stripped to their underwear, chained together, and marched to the local police station in Jayapura, is an example of how security forces enforce a pattern of denying Papuan men the status of education and of civilised masculinity (Human Rights Watch 2011). Political activism (such as taking part in demonstrations) is integral to educated masculine identity, positioning men as 'modern' and inclined to recognise rights as well as democratic principles. However, as Papuans their political activism is typically construed by the Indonesian state as disruptive to stability and development, and therefore anti-modern.

Conditions of securitisation and insecurity compel men into positions where they stand off against soldiers or feel the need to stand up for those around them who may have experienced state violence, though only minimal activism focuses on, for example, violence experienced by Papuan women (see Komnas Perempuan 2010). Indonesian authorities sometimes construe these activities as separatist, aggressive behaviours that threaten to destabilise local conditions. What Papuan men and women may see as justifiable protest, local authorities view as another illustration of violent hyper-masculine 'tribal' behaviour. For example, when men converged on a local police station in Enarotali, in the western highlands, in December 2014, to protest about the beating of two youths by Indonesian soldiers the previous night, the police opened fire on the group, killing five young men in their high school uniforms (Human Rights Watch 2014). Racialised fear of Papuan male aggression probably contributed to the police's rash reaction to the noisy, angry crowd. Security sector overreactions to Papuan crowds are an established pattern of state violence, recurring since at least the 1998 Biak Massacre, and repeated during the Wamena incident of 6 October 2000 (mentioned above). The space of protest in Papua has become increasingly violent and militarised, and therefore seen as less appropriate for women's direct involvement.

A similar tendency to view Papuan men as dangerous and threatening was common among Indonesians in North Sulawesi, and led to Dani and other students feeling stigmatised and being subjected to heightened surveillance from local authorities and police. Views of Papuan students as primitive and uncouth result in locals denying their educational achievements, skills or aspirations to build relationships with Indonesians. Dani efforts to assert these identities have brought them into conflict with Indonesians who expect recognition of a prevailing racialised hierarchy (Munro 2013, 2015).

Looking at everyday conditions of racial stigma and violence helps to reveal the context in which educated men might be striving to position themselves as 'modern' men—endeavours that occur in relation to the presence and views of Indonesians. Acts of violence towards women, intoxication (and violence), acts of protest, in addition to stereotypical views of cultural practices, affirm Indonesian views of Papuans as primitive and uncouth, and avoiding these stereotypes becomes a defining part and clear objective of being a 'modern' man. Desires, if tentative and contingent, to be non-violent, egalitarian, progressive, town-dwelling, educated men, and to eschew stigmas of primitive masculinity, require controlling appearances and how they are seen by others. There is a danger that development interventions may easily tread in the worn pathways of stigmatising men as primitive and violent if they fail to recognise the ways that some men are aspiring to embrace and practice different ways of relating to women and different ways of being men. Similarly, a too easy connection between 'tradition', gender violence and inequality downplays the modern context of violence and abuse in Wamena and other locales. The limitations placed around men's social, political and economic achievements that generate frustrations, jealousies and concerns, may exist in tandem with progressive views and practices, not least because of the need to articulate masculinity in relation to change, or one's temporal positioning in 'real-time', not the 'stone-age'.

Conclusion

In this chapter I have focused on educated highlands men who are perceived to represent a tribal masculinity of the past, and who are struggling through economic inequalities and political repression. Looking at how educated men engage with issues such as domestic violence, marriage, female education, and social/political activism reveals ways that they accept, express, or even embrace equalising gender constructs and practices. These ideas have less to do with educational attainment per se, and only marginally represent the penetration of development interventions on gender norms and rights, which are not widespread in Papua or likely to be sufficiently localised to make an impact. But ideas are not always translated into practice. Yohannes does get drunk and hit his wife. Men like, but also unlike, women are constrained by social and economic structures and gender roles and relations within the family and beyond (Eves 2006; Spark 2010). Living with political violence, racial stigma, lack of health rights (or as Lusby, this volume, discusses, legitimised violence) helps to sediment violence, hierarchy and gender inequalities into everyday life. Even when men pursue 'modern' gender relations in the high-stakes context of avoiding being seen as 'of the stone-age', these possibilities may be thwarted before they gain traction. Expressing, promoting and trying to put into practice ideas that underpin important aspects of gender equality is a path by which men may seek to position themselves as modern, righteous and innovative in a highly stigmatising and violent environment. These intentions can be supported by acknowledging and asking sensitive questions about state violence and racial stigma, and by making pathways to equality less of a struggle.

References

Alua, Agus A. 2006. 'Ap Kaintek Model Kepemimpinan Masyarakat Hubula di Lembah Balim, Papua'. In *Nilai-Nilai Hidup Masyarakat Hubula di Lembah Balim Papua* (2nd edn), ed. Nico A. Lokobal, Agus A. Alua, Thadeus N. Mulait, pp. 139–65. Jayapura: Biro Penelitian Sekolah Tinggi Filsafat Fajar Timur.

Bainton, Nicholas A. 2008, 'Men of *kastom* and the customs of men: Status, legitimacy and persistent values in Lihir, Papua New Guinea'. *The Australian Journal of Anthropology* 19(2): 194–212. doi. org/10.1111/j.1835-9310.2008.tb00122.x.

Bertrand, Jacques. 2014. 'Autonomy and stability: The perils of implementation and 'divide-and-rule' tactics in Papua, Indonesia'. *Nationalism and Ethnic Politics* 20(2): 174–99. doi.org/10.1080/1353 7113.2014.909157.

Brison, Karen. 1995. 'Changing constructions of masculinity in a Sepik society'. In *Politics of Culture in the Pacific Islands*, part II. Special Issue: *Ethnology* 34(3) (Summer): 155–75. doi.org/10.2307/3773820.

Butt, Leslie. 2015. 'Living in HIV-land: Mobility and seropositivity in highlands Papua'. In *From 'Stone Age' to 'Real Time': Exploring Papuan Temporalities, Mobilities, and Religiosities*, ed. Martin Slama and Jenny Munro, pp. 221–42. Canberra: ANU Press. Online: press.anu.edu. au/publications/series/monographs-anthropology/stone-age-real-time (accessed 24 August 2016).

——. 2005. 'Sexuality, the state, and the runaway wives of highlands Papua, Indonesia'. In *Sex in Development: Science, Sexuality, and Morality in Global Perspective*, ed. Vincanne Adams and Stacy Leigh Pigg, pp. 163–85. Durham: Duke University Press. doi. org/10.1215/9780822386414-008.

——. 2001. 'KB kills: Political violence, birth control, and the Baliem Valley Dani'. *The Asia Pacific Journal of Anthropology* 2(1): 63–86.

Butt, Leslie and Jenny Munro. 2007. 'Rebel girls? Unplanned pregnancy and colonialism in highlands Papua, Indonesia'. *Culture, Health & Sexuality* 9(6): 585–98. doi.org/10.1080/13691050701515324.

Chauvel, Richard. 2011. 'Policy failure and political impasse: Papua and Jakarta a decade after the "Papuan Spring"'. In *Comprehending West Papua*, ed. Peter King, Jim Elmslie and Camellia Webb-Gannon, pp. 105–15. Centre of Peace and Conflict Studies. Sydney: University of Sydney.

Cox, John and Martha Macintyre. 2014. 'Christian marriage, money scams, and Melanesian social imaginaries'. *Oceania* 84(2): 138–57. doi.org/10.1002/ocea.5048.

Elmhirst, Rebecca. 2007. 'Tigers and gangsters: Masculinities and feminised migration in Indonesia'. *Population, Space and Place* 13(3): 225–38. doi.org/10.1002/psp.435.

Eves, Richard. 2006. *Exploring the Role of Men and Masculinities in Papua New Guinea in the 21st Century: How to Address Violence in Ways that Generate Empowerment for Both Men and Women.* Report for Caritas Australia. Online: xyonline.net/sites/default/files/Eves,%20Exploring%20role%20of%20men%20PNG.pdf (accessed 17 November 2016).

Farhadian, Charles Edward. 2003. 'Comparing conversions among the Dani of Irian Jaya'. In *The Anthropology of Religious Conversion*, ed. Andrew Buckser and Stephen D. Glazier, pp. 55–68. Oxford: Rowman & Littlefield.

——. 2001. 'Raising the morning star: A social and ethnographic history of urban Dani Christians in New Order Indonesia'. PhD dissertation. Boston University.

Gardner, Robert and Karl Heider. 1968. *Gardens of War: Life and Death in the New Guinea Stone Age.* London: Deutsch.

Hernawan, Budi. 2015. 'Torture as a mode of governance: Reflections on the phenomenon of torture in Papua, Indonesia'. In *From 'Stone Age' to 'Real Time': Exploring Papuan Temporalities, Mobilities, and Religiosities,* ed. Martin Slama and Jenny Munro, pp. 195–220. Canberra: ANU Press. Online: press.anu.edu.au/publications/series/monographs-anthropology/stone-age-real-time (accessed 24 August 2016).

Human Rights Watch. 2014. 'Indonesia: Security forces kill five in Papua'. Online: www.hrw.org/news/2014/12/10/indonesia-security-forces-kill-five-papua (accessed 9 September 2016).

——. 2011. 'Indonesia: Independent investigation needed into Papua violence'. Online: www.hrw.org/news/2011/10/28/indonesia-independent-investigation-needed-papua-violence (accessed 9 September 2016).

Jolly, Margaret. 2008. 'Moving masculinities: Memories and bodies across Oceania'. *The Contemporary Pacific* 20(1): 1–24. doi.org/10.1353/cp.2008.0010.

Jones, Gavin W. 2005. 'The "flight from marriage" in South-east and East Asia'. *Journal of Comparative Family Studies* 36(1) (Winter): 93–119.

Kempf, Wolfgang. 2002. 'The politics of incorporation: masculinity, spatiality and modernity among the Ngaing of Papua New Guinea'. *Oceania* 73(1): 56–77.

Kirksey, Eben. 2012. *Freedom in Entangled Worlds: West Papua and the Architecture of Global Power*. Durham, NC: Duke University Press. doi.org/10.1215/9780822394761.

Knauft, Bruce M. 2011. 'Men, modernity and Melanesia'. In *Echoes of the Tambaran: Masculinity, History and the Subject in the Work of Donald F. Tuzin*, ed. David Lipset and Paul Roscoe, pp. 103–114. Canberra: ANU E Press. Online: press.anu.edu.au/publications/series/monographs-anthropology/echoes-tambaran (accessed 24 August 2016).

Komnas Perempuan. 2010. *Stop sudah! Kesaksian perempuan Papua korban kekerasan dan pelanggaran HAM, 1963–2009*. Komnas Perempuan, Pokja Perempuan Majelis Rakyat Papua. Jakarta: International Center for Transitional Justice.

Li, Tania Murray. 1999. 'Compromising power: Development, culture, and rule in Indonesia'. *Cultural Anthropology* 14(3): 295–322. doi.org/10.1525/can.1999.14.3.295.

Lusby, Stephanie. 2014. 'Preventing violence at home, allowing violence in the workplace: A case study of security guards in Papua New Guinea'. State Society and Government in Melanesia, in brief 2014/49. Canberra: The Australian National University.

Macintyre, Martha. 2012. 'Gender violence in Melanesia and the problem of Millennium Development Goal No. 3'. In *Engendering Violence in Papua New Guinea*, ed. Margaret Jolly, Christine Stewart with Carolyn Brewer, pp. 239–66. Canberra: ANU E Press. Online: press.anu.edu.au/publications/engendering-violence-papua-new-guinea (accessed 23 August 2016).

Martin, Keir. 2013. *The Death of the Big Men and the Rise of the Big Shots: Custom and Conflict in East New Britain*. New York and Oxford: Berghan Books.

Mote, Octovianus and Danilyn Rutherford. 2001. 'From Irian Jaya to Papua: The limits of primordialism in Indonesia's troubled east'. *Indonesia* 72 (October): 115–40. doi.org/10.2307/3351483.

Munro, Jenny. 2015, '"Now we know shame": *Malu* and stigma among highlanders in the Papuan diaspora'. In *From 'Stone Age' to 'Real Time': Exploring Papuan Temporalities, Mobilities, and Religiosities,* ed. Martin Slama and Jenny Munro, pp. 169–94. Canberra: ANU Press. Online: press.anu.edu.au/publications/series/monographs-anthropology/stone-age-real-time (accessed 24 August 2016).

——. 2014. 'Papuan perspectives on family planning, fertility and birth control'. State, Society and Government in Melanesia, discussion paper 2014/7. Canberra: The Australian National University.

——. 2013. 'The violence of inflated possibilities: Education, transformation and diminishment in Wamena, Papua'. *Indonesia* 95(April): 25–46.

——. 2012. '"A diploma and a descendant!" Premarital sexuality, education, and politics among Dani university students in North Sulawesi, Indonesia'. *Journal of Youth Studies* 15(8): 1011–1027. doi.org/10.1080/13676261.2012.693592.

Munro, Jenny and Patricio Wetipo. 2013. *Prevalensi minuman lokal di Wamena, Papua: laporan hasil diskusi dan rekomendasi dari masyarakat.* Online: www.academia.edu/5482245/Prevalensi_Minuman_Lokal_di_Wamena_Papua_Laporan_Awal (accessed 24 August 2016).

Naylor, Larry Lee. 1974. 'Culture change and development in the Balim Valley, Irian Jaya, Indonesia'. PhD dissertation, Southern Illinois University.

Nilan, Pam. 2009. 'Contemporary masculinities and young men in Indonesia'. *Indonesia and the Malay World* 37(109): 327–44. doi.org/10.1080/13639810903269318.

Robinson, Katherine. 2000. 'Indonesian women: from Orde Baru to Reformasi'. In *Women in Asia: Tradition, Modernity and Globalisation,* ed. Louise Edwards and Mina Roces, pp. 139–69. St Leonards: Allen & Unwin.

Slama, Martin. 2015. 'Papua as an Islamic frontier: Preaching in "the jungle" and the multiplicity of spatio-temporal hierarchisations'. In *From 'Stone Age' to 'Real Time': Exploring Papuan Temporalities, Mobilities, and Religiosities*, ed. Martin Slama and Jenny Munro, pp. 243–70. Canberra: ANU Press. Online: press.anu.edu.au/publications/series/monographs-anthropology/stone-age-real-time (accessed 24 August 2016).

Slama, Martin and Jenny Munro. 2015. 'Exploring Papuan temporalities, mobilities and religiosities: An introduction'. In *From 'Stone Age' to 'Real Time': Exploring Papuan Temporalities, Mobilities, and Religiosities*, ed. Martin Slama and Jenny Munro, pp. 1–38. Canberra: ANU Press. Online: press.anu.edu.au/publications/series/monographs-anthropology/stone-age-real-time (accessed 24 August 2016).

Slama, Martin and Jenny Munro (eds). 2015. *From 'Stone Age' to 'Real Time': Exploring Papuan Temporalities, Mobilities, and Religiosities*. Canberra: ANU Press. Online: press.anu.edu.au/publications/series/monographs-anthropology/stone-age-real-time (accessed 24 August 2016).

Spark, Ceridwen. 2010. 'Changing lives: Understanding the barriers that confront educated women in Papua New Guinea'. *Australian Feminist Studies* 25(63): 17–30. doi.org/10.1080/08164640903499901.

Stasch, Rupert. 2015. 'From primitive other to Papuan self: Korowai engagement with ideologies of unequal human worth in encounters with tourists, state officials, and education'. In *From 'Stone Age' to 'Real Time': Exploring Papuan Temporalities, Mobilities, and Religiosities*, ed. Martin Slama and Jenny Munro, pp. 59–94. Canberra: ANU Press. Online: press.anu.edu.au/publications/series/monographs-anthropology/stone-age-real-time (accessed 24 August 2016).

Taylor, John P. 2008. 'The social life of rights: "gender antagonism", modernity and raet in Vanuatu'. *The Australian Journal of Anthropology* 19(2): 165–78.

2. GENDER STRUGGLES OF EDUCATED MEN IN THE PAPUAN HIGHLANDS

Timmer, Jaap. 2015. 'Papua coming of age: The cycle of man's civilisation and two other Papuan histories'. In *From 'Stone Age' to 'Real Time': Exploring Papuan Temporalities, Mobilities, and Religiosities*, ed. Martin Slama and Jenny Munro, pp. 95–124. Canberra: ANU Press. press. anu.edu.au/publications/series/monographs-anthropology/stone-age-real-time (accessed 24 August 2016).

Wakerkwa, Feryana. 2015. 'Does empowerment really achieve the goal of improving women's lives in Papua and West Papua?' Paper presented at the Pacific Research Colloquium, The Australian National University, Canberra, January–February 2015.

Wardlow, Holly. 2006. *Wayward Women: Sexuality and Agency in a New Guinea Society*. Berkeley: University of California Press.

3

Kindy and grassroots gender transformations in Solomon Islands

John Cox
The Australian National University

Introduction

Very often in Solomon Islands and other Melanesian countries, ideas of equality between men and women are represented as inherently foreign and incompatible with *kastom*, the venerable set of social norms that include assemblages of Christian and neotraditional practices and ideals (Douglas 2003; George 2012; Jolly 2000; McDougall 2014). The opposition of women's rights and Melanesian culture is not simply the position of Melanesian traditionalists but is also reproduced by human rights advocates (cf. Hermkens 2013; Monson 2013). This dichotomous reading of complex social phenomena fails to recognise that feminism is hardly a taken-for-granted part of Western culture and that any advances in women's rights in the West or elsewhere are the result of ideological and political struggles that stretch over centuries, taking different forms in different times and places. It also ignores the diverse ways that Melanesian women are engaging with modernity and the initiatives that they are taking to improve their position in society and to make their relationships with men more equal and less prone to violence. As Martha Macintyre puts it: 'Attempts to divide women into "westernized" and "traditional" are usually reactionary ploys to discredit the political goals of women' (2000: 167).

In this chapter, I reflect on a recent and short (eight-day) visit to North Vella Lavella, a relatively under-developed part of Western Province in Solomon Islands. My purpose is to draw attention to some small-scale initiatives of women (and men) in rural Melanesia that show proactive (albeit contested) engagements with processes of changing gender relations there. The point is not to romanticise grassroots development by claiming that the kindergarten described provides a model of transformative feminist praxis. Rather, by bringing a humble village kindergarten into view, I hope to open up more options for thinking about the dynamics of social change in Solomon Islands and to unsettle the commonly accepted view that ideologies of male dominance are supported by *kastom* and are so firmly entrenched in rural areas as to be uncontestable.

Surprising connections in out of the way places

In November 2014, The Australian National University mobilised several research teams to observe the national elections in Solomon Islands (Cox 2015a). I was a mentor to five Solomon Islanders in the North Vella Lavella Constituency. Vella Lavella is the most north-western of the large islands in the New Georgia Group in Western Province. It is home to some 10,000 people, with about 4,000 living in North Vella. Vella was a heavily contested battlefield during World War II and much of the island's transportation infrastructure dates from that period, including the roads and airstrip in South Vella. The southern half of Vella is close to markets in Gizo, the provincial capital, and so provides better opportunities for cash income than in the North. There is some small-scale cultivation of cocoa and copra, but most who live on Vella rely on subsistence gardening and fishing. Logging companies operate on the island, generating more conflict between clans than payment of royalties (Berg 2008). Formal sector employment is limited to clergy, school teachers and the nurse aids who staff the dilapidated village aid posts. Anyone seriously ill is transported by canoe to Gizo Hospital.

Our election observation team for North Vella was the only all-male research team, which concerned me as I felt this would limit our access to women's views, even though we surveyed an equal number of women and men during the campaign period and on polling day. This concern was borne out in a number of awkward interviews that I did with (especially younger) women who were painfully shy and who offered only the most minimal answers to our questions. Nevertheless, as is often the case in this type of activity, other unexpected connections and informal relationships that developed in the field provided more access and insight than were elicited by the formal research tools we were using. Similarly, while our explicit purpose was to observe political activities and the formal processes of voting and counting votes, we also had a mandate to contextualise these activities by making wider enquiries and observations. In my case, this included broader questions about economic activity, service delivery, local governance and gender relations.

Arriving in one of the North Vella villages for our pre-poll surveying, our team was introduced to one of several local chiefs, the United Church pastor and the principal of the community high school. These could be seen as three male leadership roles that reflect a commonly perceived set of moral fields in Melanesia: *kastom* (traditional culture), *lotu* (Christianity) and *gavman* (the state and its institutions) (Barker 2007; Burridge 1995; Cox 2015b). The principal and I made eye contact (did he look familiar?) and I introduced myself, shaking hands. He introduced himself as 'Daniel' and asked, 'John, what is your second name?' I replied, 'John Cox' (using my full name because in Solomon Islands I am often known as 'John Cox', spoken as if it were one word). 'I thought so!' he responded. In the subsequent conversations over several days we pieced together the various times we had met over the last decade or longer. The most recent encounter was in 2005 when I had interviewed him in Gizo as part of a project evaluation I was doing as a consultant to the Australian Red Cross. Prior to that, we had met in various schools at which he had taught and where I had placed volunteers as a program manager for Australian Volunteers International, notably Vonunu Provincial Secondary School on South Vella Lavella. Our connections encompassed many of my various engagements with Solomon Islands since my first visit in 1998 and the development of Daniel's own career in education in a number of locations around Western Province.

I was surprised to find someone that I knew in such an out of the way place but as we talked over the next several days, I was also reminded of how cosmopolitan rural Solomon Islands can be (McDougall 2016) and has always been, with layered interconnections between the islands predating (and intensifying during) the colonial period (Bennett 1987; Dureau 2013; Hviding 2014). Daniel, the community high school principal, has worked in a number of government and church schools around Western Province and, although he lives in a village with few services that is some distance (2–3 hours by outboard motor canoe) from Gizo, he is well connected and well informed, particularly about the education sector. Since leaving Vella, I have had some contact with Daniel by SMS and Facebook, to the extent that he has reviewed a draft of this chapter. These communications are only possible when he visits Gizo or Honiara due to poor connectivity in the village. In this, he is not atypical of other educated villagers. I spoke to several pastors and retired teachers who had worked all over Western Province and in Honiara and who kept up their external connections, including with former Australian volunteers, through letters and mobile phone communication. Many have adult children working in Honiara who send through phone credits or cash to facilitate these links.

A village kindy

During my stay on North Vella, I was invited to a 'closing ceremony', marking the end of the teaching year for the village 'kindy' (kindergarten), run by Daniel's bright and energetic wife Evelyn. Although this was not central to our election observation brief, I thought it would be ill-mannered to refuse the invitation. I also hoped that by attending I might get a better feel for how some basic services are delivered in the electorate. The closing ceremony was to be held at the United Church, the largest building in the village. As I entered, I realised this was a big event. The church was full, with about 100 people there, including dozens of small children, their older siblings and proud mothers and fathers. I snuck into the back, trying to be as inconspicuous as possible and hoping simply to observe the proceedings. However, I was soon summoned to sit at the front with the village leadership: the aforementioned community high school principal, pastor and chiefs and the three women who run the kindy. The school chaplain was giving a sermon in Pidjin and English (but not Bilua, the vernacular language of Vella (Berg 2008: 39), nor Roviana, the language of Methodism in the Western Solomons (McDougall 2012).

This choice of languages is not uncommon. The Sunday worship service I had attended in another village a few days earlier was also conducted in a mix of Pidjin and English, languages that index a register of national and international value, not least that of modern education (Demian 2015).

Soon I was on my feet handing out prizes to about 40 small children, each of whom was called up by name and made to shake my hand before receiving their bag of sweets. The various classes then performed for an audience of parents and relatives, singing songs and reciting poems, the days of the week and months of the year. With prompting from the three women kindy teachers, all of this was done in English. On the one hand, this was cute and appealing. Yet, at another level, by showing off their early adoption of English, the children were performing the modernising value of early childhood education (Glasgow et al. 2011; Jourdan 2007).

Clearly some in the village were not entirely convinced of the need for this new level of schooling (Burton 2012; cf. the male disparagement of women's groups documented by Dureau 1993; McDougall 2016: 117). I had already sensed that some local micro-politics were in play and that I had been conscripted onto the side of education. Therefore I was not entirely surprised when Daniel, who was acting as master of ceremonies, announced to everyone that I was going to give a speech on 'early childhood education'. Those who know me laugh when they hear this story, as there are many others with a much higher level of interest in this topic than me (to say the least). Nevertheless, I knew the kind of thing I should say and so found the words to tell the crowd how I had benefited from two years of kindergarten and a mother who read to me in bed as a small child. Daniel seemed pleased with my performance.

Over the generous feast they had prepared for lunch, I learned just how new the kindy was. Systems for supporting kindergartens and training for teachers of early childhood education have been irregular in Solomon Islands. While some kindy teachers have studied at the University of the South Pacific campus in Honiara, the Solomon Islands College of Higher Education began its first diploma in Early Childhood Education in 2009 as part of a major reform of the sector (Kelly, Daiwo and Malasa 2011). This was only the third year of operation for the North Vella kindy. It has no external funding and the three teachers volunteer their time, even as they are each working on distance-education courses to obtain diplomas in early childhood education. The kindy teachers are all women and two of the three are married to teachers at the community high school or primary school. Their husbands are highly supportive of their efforts, often a precondition of success in this kind of environment (Sharp et al. 2015; Spark 2011). In neighbouring villages, news of the kindy has spread and some are thinking about starting their own versions of it. However, thinking about something does not necessarily translate into outcomes and I admired the vision, endeavour and perseverance of my hosts.

That evening, I went up to Daniel's house for dinner. As my colleague and I talked with him, his wife Evelyn (the leader of the kindy), prepared food for us and marshalled children, despite being exhausted from a long day organising the closing ceremony, for which she had also cooked food. I felt rather guilty for not offering to assist in lightening my hostess's 'triple burden' and for making it impossible for her husband to assist her (Pollard 2003). I felt guilty again after dinner for asking her questions about gender issues in Vella. However, I had wanted to speak to her as one of the few educated women that I had access to during my time there and she had agreed to talk with me.

Development and clientelism

I found the story of the kindy inspiring. Believing in the importance of early childhood education, Evelyn had decided to start a group at her own house and without any funding or resourcing from elsewhere: 'a sole inspirational champion' as Lindsay Burton (2012: 168) describes the chair of a Makira kindergarten. As interest grew, Evelyn enlisted two other teachers and all three of them have started their certificates in early childhood education by distance learning through the Solomon Islands National University (until recently, the Solomon Islands College of Higher Education). This initiative has happened with the support of her husband, the most senior education official in the village, and moves are in place to allow the kindy to be recognised by the Ministry of Education, which will make it eligible for some limited funding. Alice Pollard writes:

> many [Solomon Islands] women are visionary and want to implement their vision within their own language or cultural group or with whom they share a common interest such as religious affiliation. Generally they prefer to do so on a voluntary basis (Pollard 2003: 56).

The kindy certainly exemplifies the capacity of women in rural Solomon Islands to implement their vision locally. However, I believe the voluntary origins of the kindy reflect the limited resources currently available, not the preference for unpaid work that Pollard assumes. In fact, Evelyn was taking steps to formalise and professionalise the kindy by improving her own and her assistants' education standards. She also hoped to become eligible for Ministry of Education funding, even though fully staffed and funded village kindergartens are an unlikely prospect for the time being.

In some ways, the village kindy exemplifies the principles of (neoliberal) participatory development. In the absence of the state, people use their own resources to identify and meet their own needs. However, 'communities' are rarely the innocent and cohesive social groups often assumed by development practitioners (Foale 2001). Here the unspoken subtext was that many of the senior men of the village (and perhaps more conservative women) were a little uncomfortable with women taking the initiative and introducing a new institution over which the men had no control. While child-rearing is routinely understood as women's work, education is a field of public social advancement that bears upon questions of male prestige (McKeown 2001). Hence the need for a legitimating public performance of the value of the kindy that co-opted not only visiting researchers but also village leadership. Held in the village church, the ceremony also included the village pastor and the (well-educated) chaplain of the community high school. The closing ceremony marked the kindy as a key enabler of modern Christian education, something no one could oppose without marking themselves as ignorant, backward or faithless, or perhaps *lokol*, a Pidjin term of disparagement for those unable to communicate in Pidjin or English (McDougall 2012).

Solomon Islands is a country characterised by very low standards of literacy, even when compared to other Pacific Islands countries. Historically, women there have been excluded from the education system (Strachan 2009). The Ministry of Education and Human Resources Development (MEHRD) reports its disappointment at the very low rates of participation in early childhood education across the country and notes that these are falling behind population growth. If kindergartens are growing rapidly in Solomon Islands (Kelly, Daiwo and Malasa 2011), they are not growing fast enough to meet the needs of a very young population. Nevertheless, given the historic neglect of girls' education, the relatively even participation of girls and boys in kindergartens—girls numbered 48.5 percent of kindergarten enrolments in 2013—is encouraging (MEHRD 2013: 22).

In the context of decades of poor service delivery in Solomon Islands and the increasing transfer of public monies into the hands of political patrons, initiating anything new that presumes a public good can be controversial. Politicians may even see themselves as in competition with development programs and they—or their local agents—may see those who seek to improve services as a political threat (Cox 2009). This is because the legitimacy of political patrons is now tied to the normalisation of very low expectations of development. Development in Solomon Islands is not a vision of a prosperous economy or well-resourced schools and hospitals. Rather, it is being redefined as petty political patronage: outboard motors, roofing iron and other minor benefits that are accessed by individuals or heads of households at the whim of politicians or their committees. Other payments may include school fees and medical costs or, particularly around elections, a bag of rice or other small gifts of food or cash. Our observation team heard a number of stories of this nature. Politicians may be criticised as unfair or niggardly distributors of these particularistic benefits but the idea that the MP's primary role is that of distribution is now deeply embedded in Solomon Islands political culture (Cox 2015a).

It was not at all clear from our research on the elections that there was much if any concern about gender inequality in North Vella (Scheyvens 2003; Soaki, this volume). Both men and women expressed little interest in our questions about women standing for election, a hypothetical possibility in a constituency where four men were competing against each other. A number of women indicated that they would be happy for good women candidates to stand in the future but that they would not be likely to vote for them. I interpret this kind of apparently perverse answer as a performance of loyal clientelist citizenship. The women who participated in our surveys were expected to vote for the (male) candidates supported by their families or husbands. Therefore they would not wish to answer questions in ways that could imply disloyalty to a family patron, nor that would imply that they themselves were dishonest: promising to vote for one candidate but telling an interviewer that they would prefer to vote for someone else. In this context of pervasive clientelism, I found Evelyn's commitment to the kindy remarkable. Indeed, it was the only thing happening on North Vella that looked, to my eyes, like 'development'.

The subversive kindy and changing gender roles

> It will be admitted that a man of slight education and meagre powers can actually teach all that the native, in his present state, needs to know; but when so much depends upon how that little is taught, we see the necessity of the most thorough training. The Pacific is, in reality, only a kindergarten, and its best institutions are only schools for children; but we are recognizing to-day that it needs the best brain to teach children, if they are to reap the fullest advantages of education (Burton 1912: 274).

As the above quotation exemplifies, early missionaries regarded education through a highly condescending and racialised set of beliefs about civilisation. Nevertheless, their flawed interventions—often based around ideas of 'child rescue'—established much of the educational infrastructure within the region (Young 1989). Although the Methodist Mission established a network of kindergartens in the Western District before World War II (Gina 2003), the oldest kindergarten still operating in Solomon Islands is the YWCA kindy in Honiara. YWCA has a long history of promoting the empowerment of women and girls across the country and the Pacific region, although in Solomon Islands the organisation has only had offices in Honiara and in Munda, Western Province. In the late 1970s, the establishment of YWCA in Munda initially drew considerable resistance from male politicians and the United Church, who saw it as a threat to their own women's groups (Feary and Lai 2012: 45ff). However, these divisions were resolved long ago and YWCA is now very much an accepted part of the church and broader community. Since 1982, YWCA has also run a kindergarten in Munda, which may have influenced Evelyn, as she is a United Church member and has family and work connections to the Munda area.

In speaking with Evelyn, it became apparent that the scope of her work was not merely about giving children in a poorly serviced part of Solomon Islands the opportunity for improved educational outcomes (Gould 2000). Nor was Evelyn motivated by the desire to socialise children into a national polity (Glasgow 2011; Jourdan 1995; Munro 2013) or a transnational middle class (Brison 2009). Other elements of her work that Evelyn explained to me included a broader vision of renewed gender relations quite subversive of the normative hierarchy where women and girls are presumed to be subordinate to men and boys. Solomon Islands girls are widely thought to have no need to learn English if it is expected that they will grow up to be village women whose role is not to busy themselves with the decisions of men but to rear children and work in homes and gardens (Dureau 1993).

In this kindy, Evelyn insists that there are no gendered activities, boys and girls do everything together and cooperatively. Evelyn's model of childhood behaviour matches Karen Brison's (2009) description of village kindergartens in Fiji, where gendered divisions between children are not pronounced. Rather than simply regarding the absence of gendered distinctions among young children as a natural state, Evelyn seeks to establish more durable patterns of equitable gender relations. She hopes that this grounding will stay with them as they progress through higher levels of education. She explicitly intends the kindy to provide a formative experience of gender equality and respect for adult women that will shape children, particularly boys, for the rest of their lives.

Kindergartens in Solomon Islands have previously been identified as places where gendered identities can be reformed (e.g. Donnelly 2008). However, the focus of Solomon Islands feminist thinking in the past has been less about reshaping the masculinity of boys and more about liberating women from incessant childcare and allowing them time for work or other interests (Makini 1989; Pollard 2000: 17).

Evelyn's practice is consonant with the growing international interest in working with men to nurture non-violent masculinities that respect women. Her hope that 'when the boys grow up and become men with their own families, they will look after their wives' reflects her attempt to nurture a gentler, more respectful version of masculinity in Solomon Islands. Indeed, the approval and active support given to Evelyn by her husband Daniel indicates that this gentler, more respectful masculinity is already taking shape (Cox and Macintyre 2014). Evelyn's hopes may be better grounded in a kindy run by women where children come to experience women as intelligent leaders than in general village life or in other levels of schooling where the presence of male teachers is likely to provide a different model of gender relations.

Gender equality, human rights and global cultural flows

Educated women in urban areas of Melanesia are often regarded as having difficult challenges to face as they try to break out of a conservative set of social constraints that are imagined to characterise Melanesian culture (Macintyre 2011; Spark 2011). Therefore, to find a project like Evelyn's kindy in rural Solomon Islands, particularly one being developed so independently of any external interventions, was surprising. Evelyn and Daniel may not fit popular (and often academic) stereotypes of rural people, in that they are educated and have personal and professional networks that extend well beyond the village context. Perhaps they are more characteristic of the nascent regional middle class (Barbara, Cox and Leach 2015; Brison 2009). And yet their interconnectedness with wider social worlds also characterises more rural people than is often presumed, particularly in Western Solomon Islands (Hviding 2014; McDougall 2016).

Evelyn and Daniel provide an example of the kind of dissemination of global flows of images and ideas, expectations and aspirations, consumer goods and modern dispositions that Charles Taylor has suggested flow into broader society after first being adopted by small circles of elites (Taylor 2004). Indeed, flows of global modernity, particularly those mediated through Christian traditions, do also include ideals of gender equity, albeit inconsistently and in ways that are contested or simply contradicted by other images and practices (Jolly 2000). These changes take place over long periods of time and in Melanesia have a direct lineage that goes back to missionary practices during the colonial era (Dureau 1993; McDougall 2014; Young 1989).

With Macintyre, I have argued that gender relations in Melanesia are changing as a result of such dynamics. In Papua New Guinea, middle-class Pentecostal Christians have cultivated new ideals and practices of marriage that have set a new norm of modern living, initially within a relatively elite group but currently circulating more widely (Cox and Macintyre 2014). Melanesian Christian ideals of marriage also now include nucleated families and companionate romance. These models have implications for the ways men reimagine the standing of their wives and recognise their personhood (Brison 2009; Langmore 1989; Wardlow 2006).

In the case of the United Church of Solomon Islands there is a formal recognition of the equality of men and women, even though this is hardly reflected in everyday practice (Dureau 1993; Munro, this volume). Nevertheless, from time to time, men may experience personal religious convictions that impel them to reconcile the dissonance between their own behaviour and official church views of proper Christian conduct (Cox and Macintyre 2014). An example of this from the Western Solomons is the (Roviana- and Methodist-born) first Speaker of Parliament, Lloyd Maepeza Gina, who, in his autobiography, thinks it important to recount how his mid-life evangelical reawakening led him to a positive and more respectful revaluing of his wife and family (Gina 2003). Perhaps over-optimistically, I read such professions not as self-serving justifications that mask underlying violence and male privilege, but as rearticulations of social norms that are slowly displacing old ways and making overt male dominance less morally respectable.

Debra McDougall provides another instance of these processes of change in the Western Solomons, noting the 'relatively uncontroversial' admission of women to chief's committees in Ranongga. She argues that although some men still resist human rights and women's rights as foreign intrusions that undermine *kastom*, 'the constant reiteration of the language of human rights seems to have normalised it' (2014: 203) and has allowed women to exercise new forms of leadership.

Nevertheless, feminist scholars have recognised that international human rights discourses are not straightforwardly emancipatory. They may reinscribe gendered roles that render women as victims. In so doing, women's agency is erased and the fluidity and adaptability of local cultural practices become fixed as oppressive, violent and immutable (Hermkens 2013). Echoing the preoccupations of nineteenth-century missionaries, 'culture' becomes the site of dysfunction and the explanation of why development programs are unsuccessful (Merry 2003). Advocates of women's rights then risk reinforcing a static and patriarchal understanding of local culture.

Kastom and modernity

I see Evelyn and her husband Daniel as people who selectively embrace innovations from outside the local 'cultural' world that is often supposed to circumscribe normative behaviour in Melanesia. This undermines the oppositional view of 'authentic' Melanesian *kastom* set against 'foreign' ideals of women's rights. Where popular accounts of *kastom* regard it as a primeval unchanging body of traditional practices and roles, anthropologists see in *kastom* layers of history that reflect not only Melanesian culture but the colonial experience, Christian conversion and contemporary politics. David Akin, in his magisterial study of the Maasina Rule movement, has argued that the historical experience of Malaitans in their struggles against the British colonial government has given rise to a particular ideology of *kastom* (2013). This Malaitan ideology is 'not an anachronistic longing for the past, or an attempt to preserve or revive lost traditions per se, but rather a modern and evolving political philosophy born from the colonial and postcolonial experience' (ibid.: 342).

Malaitan *kastom*, like *kastom* all over Melanesia, is therefore dynamic and political, not a nostalgic longing for past ways. *Kastom* plays out in subtly different ways around the country, not least in the ways that particular versions of *kastom* are employed to police women's behaviour and the conduct of men towards women. Malaitan *kastom* is seen by many Solomon Islanders to be more patriarchal and more insistent on sexual propriety. This can lead to disputes over matters such as bridewealth when Malaitans interact with people from other traditions. As Malaita has become a defined 'other' for many in Western Province and especially Guadalcanal, these differences have become more fixed and emblematic of the oppositional identities that have become the ideological drivers of the 1998–2003 civil unrest (Allen 2013). However, McDougall (2016: 196–207) argues that disputes over sexual improprieties and so forth are not the result of clashes between incompatible cultural systems. Rather, such disputes are common even within supposedly homogeneous groups and so conflict between Ranonggans and Malaitans is in practice resolved within comparable *kastom* frameworks.

Kastom always involves an engagement with modern ideas and systems. As Matthew Allen et al. note, '*Kastom* systems do not function independently from the other systems under discussion, including the state' (2013: 34). Indeed, as McDougall notes for Ranongga, customary institutions such as chiefs' committees are 'better viewed as the last remnant of a colonial system of indirect rule neglected by a postcolonial state' (2014: 217). *Kastom* is not always institutionalised in roles such as chiefs but is often articulated as a moral reference point. Benedicta Rousseau (2008) interprets *kastom* in Vanuatu as a mode of right conduct or a tool for the judgement of proper behaviour that incorporates Christianity and other modern institutions and situations without necessarily making a strong claim to indigeneity. She argues that, 'With few exceptions, Christian principles are viewed as a core part of indigenous identity, and previously perceived incompatibilities between *kastom* and Christianity have been ironed out (or at least smoothed over)' (2008: 16). This 'ironing out' or 'smoothing over' has been happening for a long time in Western Solomon Islands. Part of this integration of an older indigenous tradition with Christianity has included a very active acceptance of modern education.

Rights, education and culture

Contemporary ideas and practices of education, particularly early childhood education, contain an implied gender equality in their commitment to developing the modern social and educational skills of individual children even as they inculcate social norms that index a global middle class (Brison 2009). This is not to deny the pervasive practices in society at large that discriminate against women and girls, not least in educational systems. Brison (2009), for example, argues that middle-class kindergartens in urban Fiji intensify the processes by which children come to identify with stereotypical gender roles for girls and boys. These serious injustices notwithstanding (or perhaps because of them), the underlying principles of gender equity seem to be visible, intelligible and attractive to at least some women in rural Solomon Islands. Some are finding ways of acting out ideals of gender equity as they also strive to achieve other objectives. Rather than seeing villages as bastions of pre-modern tradition—particularly as places of immutable misogynist tradition where the very idea of gender equality is a foreign imposition fundamentally irreconcilable with local cultural norms—academics, development practitioners and advocates for gender equity should be conscious of the ways in which global cultural flows are being appropriated by women and men in unlikely places and with potentially transformative effects.

Burton (2012) has documented a project of cultural rejuvenation through early childhood education in Makira Province. Her research examines a successful kindergarten, run by members of the South Seas Evangelical Church (SSEC) and grounded in respect for indigenous values. The SSEC kindy is one way in which its community are responding to their anxieties of 'intergenerational cultural decay' in the face of economic change (Tepahae 1997). Burton contrasts the SSEC kindergarten with a kindy in a Church of Melanesia community dominated by what she sees as individualistic values that undermine cultural values and communitarian efforts to maintain a public good. This is a somewhat surprising finding given the historical predisposition of the Church of Melanesia to incorporate indigenous culture and language into worship (Hilliard 1978). The SSEC, by contrast, have tended to be more explicitly committed to (Christian) modernisation, often hostile to traditional practices and active in their use of English and Pidjin (Watson-Gegeo and Gegeo 1991).

The colonial and postcolonial history of Western Province is quite different from that of Malaita or Makira and continues to shape the ways that Western Province people engage with modern ideas, institutions and practices. Western Province had a very different experience of labour recruiting and plantations and the Methodist and Seventh-day Adventist churches have shaped the western regional identity quite differently from the Anglicans and SSEC in the Eastern Solomons (Bennett 1987; Dureau 2008).

The North Vella kindy does not appear to exhibit the dynamics that Burton describes in cultural terms. In Vella, Western knowledge and pedagogy were not problematised, nor was there an explicit commitment to integrating Western and indigenous knowledge practices. Rather, at least in the form displayed to the village in the closing ceremony, the kindy modelled itself as an effective induction into Western schooling and particularly the modern life skills of English language, literacy, numeracy and measurement of time in days and months (Makini 1989). As far as I could tell, this was not seen as a threat to the indigenous culture of the area, perhaps because of earlier shifts within the United Church where the transition from the Methodist Mission to the United Church of Papua New Guinea and Solomon Islands (1968) expanded the scale at which the church operated from the regional Roviana-speaking Western Solomons to a transnational level where English played a more important role (Hviding 1996; McDougall 2012).

In many cases, cultural narratives of the failure of development in the Pacific founder in the face of comparative evidence (Haque 2012). Such narratives are not always imposed from the outside. They can also be seen as ideological products of indigenous elites who have already captured the benefits of education and other services and economic opportunities and seek to justify their position by arguing that the 'innocent population' of Melanesian subsistence horticulturalists has no real need of such Western impositions (Golub 2014; Hau'ofa 1987). These views often entail condescending and oppressive views of the place of women in society and may seek to 'protect' women from the corrupting and destabilising influence of 'foreign' ideas such as women's rights or gender equity (George 2012; Taylor 2008).

In practice, Melanesians are as likely to look for ways of bringing the modern and the cultural together as to insist that the two are opposed. One evening, Daniel asked me what I thought of human rights. This was a lead into discussing the difficult issue of the corporal punishment of children, a practice officially banned in Solomon Islands schools but retaining considerable popular legitimacy. Daniel saw child rights as a part of the 'whiteman culture that is coming in, where if you beat your children I'll report you to the police'. However, this process for him was not about reinforcing a popular narrative of cultural loss or 'intergenerational cultural decay' (Burton 2012). While he contrasted 'whiteman' (Cox 2015b) and Melanesian cultures, this was at the level of practice and did not mark out two incompatible cultural domains. As far as Daniel was concerned, his society was undergoing a transition where practices were changing for the better but the process of change has created problems—such as new modes of disciplining children—that need to be addressed proactively. In his mind, these are management issues, not a fundamental clash of cultural values.

Nor was he personally threatened by the new paradigm, as some men have been (Taylor 2008). Indeed, as the quotes from Iriqila (a large village in North Vella Lavella) reproduced by Pauline Soaki (this volume) indicate, Solomon Islands women themselves often find rights discourse troubling and frame it in opposition to *kastom*. Daniel himself accepted the desirability of new non-violent practices in the school but was concerned about disciplinary issues, now that 'children don't worry because there's no big punishment' (in the absence of physical punishment). He told me about his way of managing discipline by initiating dialogues between parents, children and teachers. He saw dialogue as a means of easing tensions over different understandings of discipline as well as addressing specific aspects of children's misbehaviour while at school.

As with Evelyn's initiative in setting up the kindy, training herself and other teachers and accessing other resources, Daniel's school management practices represent a pragmatic engagement with the highly desirable good of modern education. However, this commitment does not rest on an ideological rejection of the customary as backward, primitive or sinful. If there is a cultural humiliation underlying their desire for change (Sahlins 1992), it is far from apparent. Rather, there is a curiosity and an ambivalent openness to both the customary past and the modern future (Dureau 2014). As the active involvement of chiefs and pastors in the kindy closing ceremony indicates, Daniel and Evelyn seem able to work with *kastom, lotu* and *gavman* (the three points of moral orientation outlined by Burridge 1995) in the same frame, mobilising all sources of support and validation for their developmental project. Indeed, Daniel himself is now preparing for a chiefly role within his own island community and has asked me to supply him with relevant ethnographic materials. He is particularly interested in the writings of A.M. Hocart whose 1908 research in Simbo, Vella and other islands is held to be a valuable historical resource by many contemporary Western Solomon Islanders (Hviding and Berg (eds) 2014).

Conclusion

The widespread engagement of Pacific Islanders with modern institutions, ideas and practices is recognised by anthropologists as a complex process that involves degrees of agency, encompassment, resistance and appropriation (LiPuma 2000; Sahlins 1992). If Pacific Islanders embrace modern institutions, such as Christianity or educational systems, they may do so on their own terms and for their own reasons. This does not require them to surrender their cultural integrity or make a Sisyphean commitment to inevitable failure in their repeated attempts to reconcile an essential incompatibility between indigenous and Western cultural values and ways of being.

Across the Pacific (and beyond), the flashpoints of local politics of tradition are often found in arguments about the proper place and conduct of women. These debates can appear reactionary to those who take Western liberal democratic traditions as a global norm (notwithstanding the ongoing sexism in Australia and other developed countries that are presumed to provide a model for developing states). In drawing attention to the North Vella kindergarten, my intention has been to show how ordinary Melanesians are negotiating these debates about changing gender roles. Evelyn and her husband Daniel provide examples not of feminist revolutionary activists, but of progressive educationalists who have fostered an acceptance of women's initiative in a very conservative environment. In doing so, they have gently inserted practices of gender equality into local narratives of development. They have done so without allowing their agenda to be lost in fruitless debates about *kastom* where cultural integrity is defined in ways that make women subservient to men. Rather, they have operated in the 'emerging cracks in neo-traditional forms of patriarchy' (McDougall 2014: 203). While they are hardly calculating people, their modest, shrewd and subtle means of working for change may provide something of a model for others who seek the same ends.

References

Akin, David. 2013. *Colonialism, Maasina Rule and the Origins of Malaitan Kastom*. Honolulu: University of Hawai'i Press. doi.org/10.21313/ hawaii/9780824838140.001.0001.

Allen, Matthew. 2013. *Greed and Grievance: Ex-Militants' Perspectives on the Conflict in Solomon Islands, 1998–2003*. Honolulu: University of Hawai'i Press. doi.org/10.21313/hawaii/9780824838546.001.0001.

Allen, Matthew, Sinclair Dinnen, Daniel Evans and Rebecca Monson. 2013. *Justice Delivered Locally: Systems, Challenges and Innovations in Solomon Islands*. Research Report, Justice for the Poor, New York: The World Bank.

Barbara, Julien, John Cox and Michael Leach. 2015. 'The emergent middle classes in Timor-Leste and Melanesia: Conceptual relevance and identification'. State, Society and Governance in Melanesia, discussion paper 2015/4. Canberra: The Australian National University.

Barker, John. 2007. 'All sides now: The postcolonial triangle in Uiaku'. In *The Anthropology of Morality in Melanesia and Beyond*, ed. John Barker, pp. 75–91. Aldershot and Burlington: Ashgate.

Bennett, Judith. 1987. *Wealth of the Solomons: A History of a Pacific Archipelago, 1800–1978*. Honolulu: University of Hawai'i Press.

Berg, Cato. 2008. 'A chief is a chief wherever he goes: Land and lines of power in Vella Lavella, Solomon Islands'. PhD dissertation, University of Bergen.

Brison, Karen. 2009. 'Shifting conceptions of self and society in Fijian kindergartens'. *Ethos* 37(3): 314–33. doi.org/10.1111/j.1548-1352.2009.01055.x.

Burridge, Kenelm. 1995 [1960]. *Mambu: A Melanesian Millennium.* Princeton: Princeton University Press. doi. org/10.1515/9781400851584.

Burton, John Wear. 1912. *The Call of the Pacific.* London: Charles H. Kelly.

Burton, Lindsay. 2012. 'Building on living traditions: Early childhood education and culture in Solomon Islands'. *Current Issues in Comparative Education* 15(1): 157–75.

Cox, John. 2015a. 'The politics of distribution in Solomon Islands: North Vella Lavella constituency'. State, Society and Governance in Melanesia, in brief 2015/1. Canberra: The Australian National University.

——. 2015b. 'Israeli technicians and the postcolonial racial triangle in Papua New Guinea'. *Oceania* 85(3): 342–58. doi.org/10.1002/ocea.5100.

——. 2009. 'Active citizenship or passive clientelism? Accountability and development in Solomon Islands'. *Development in Practice* 19(8): 964–80. doi.org/10.1080/09614520903220784.

Cox, John and Martha Macintyre. 2014. 'Christian marriage, money scams and Melanesian social imaginaries'. *Oceania* 84(2): 138–57. doi.org/10.1002/ocea.5048.

Demian, Melissa. 2015. 'Dislocating custom'. *Political and Legal Anthropology Review* 38(1): 91–107. doi.org/10.1111/plar.12088.

Donnelly John. 2008. *Early Childhood Education: A Solid Foundation in the Solomon Islands. The Girl Child Reading and Rescue Project.* Melbourne: World Vision Australia.

Douglas, Bronwen. 2003. 'Christianity, tradition and everyday modernity: Towards an anatomy of women's groupings in Melanesia'. *Oceania* 74(1–2): 6–23. doi.org/10.1002/j.1834-4461.2003.tb02833.x.

Dureau, Christine. 2013. 'Visibly black: Phenotype and cosmopolitan aspirations in Simbo, Western Solomon Islands'. In *Senses and Citizenships: Embodying Political Life*, ed. Susanna Trnka, Christine Dureau and Julie Park, pp. 33–54. New York and London: Routledge.

———. 2008. 'Decreed affinities: Nationhood and the Western Solomon Islands'. *Journal of Pacific History* 33(2): 197–220.

———. 1993. 'Nobody asked the mother: Women and maternity on Simbo, Western Solomon Islands'. *Oceania* 64(1): 18–35. doi. org/10.1002/j.1834-4461.1993.tb02445.x.

Feary, Sue and Jocelyn Lai. 2012. *Stori blo YWCA: A History of the Young Women's Christian Association in Solomon Islands*. Honiara: Solomon Islands YWCA.

Foale, Simon. 2001. 'Where's our development? Land-owner expectations and environmentalist agendas in Western Solomon Islands'. *The Asia Pacific Journal of Anthropology* 2(2): 44–67. doi.org/10.1080/144422 10110001706105.

George, Nicole. 2012. *Situating Women: Gender Politics and Circumstance in Fiji*. Canberra: ANU E Press. Online: press.anu.edu.au/publications/ situating-women (accessed 12 August 2016).

Gina, Lloyd Maepeza. 2003. *Journeys in a Small Canoe: The Life and Times of a Solomon Islander*. Canberra: Pandanus Press.

Glasgow, Ali. 2011. 'Curriculum development in early childhood development: Cook Islands and Solomon Islands'. In *Harvesting Ideas: Perspectives from a Niu Generation of Pacific Leaders,* ed. Kabini Sanga and Joanna Kidman, pp. 148–63. Suva: University of South Pacific Press.

Glasgow, Ali, Bernadine Ha'amori, Joanna Daiwo and Viola Malasa. 2011. 'The Solomon Islands initiatives to support and enhance the use of vernaculars in early childhood education'. *Language and Linguistics in Melanesia* 29: 87–94.

Golub, Alex. 2014. *Leviathans at the Gold Mine: Creating indigenous and corporate actors in Papua New Guinea*. Durham, NC: Duke University Press. doi.org/10.1215/9780822377399.

Gould, Diana. 2000. 'The relationship between early childhood education and primary school academic achievement in Solomon Islands'. *International Journal of Early Childhood* 32(1): 1–8. doi.org/10.1007/BF03169016.

Haque, Tobias. 2012. 'Influence of culture on economic development in Solomon Islands: A political-economy perspective'. State, Society and Governance in Melanesia, discussion paper 2012/1. Canberra: The Australian National University.

Hau'ofa, Epeli. 1987. 'The new South Pacific society: Integration and independence'. In *Class and Culture in the South Pacific*, ed. Anthony Hooper, Steve Britton, Ron Crocombe, Judith Huntsman and Cluny Macpherson, pp. 1–15. Auckland: University of Auckland and Suva: University of the South Pacific.

Hermkens, Anna-Karina. 2013. '"*Raits blong mere*"? Framing human rights and gender relations in Solomon Islands'. *Intersections: Gender and Sexuality in Asia and the Pacific* 33. Online: intersections.anu.edu.au/issue33/hermkens.htm (accessed 18 June 2016).

Hilliard, David. 1978. *God's Gentlemen: A History of the Melanesian Mission, 1849–1942*. St Lucia: University of Queensland Press.

Hviding, Edvard. 2014. 'Across the New Georgia Group: A.M. Hocart's fieldwork as inter-island practice'. In *The Ethnographic Experiment: A.M. Hocart and W.H.R. Rivers in Island Melanesia, 1908*, ed. Edvard Hviding and Cato Berg, pp. 71–107. Oxford and New York: Berghahn Books.

——. 1996. *Guardians of Marovo Lagoon: Practice, Place, and Politics in Maritime Melanesia*. Honolulu: University of Hawai'i Press.

Hviding, Edvard and Cato Berg (eds). 2014. *The Ethnographic Experiment: A.M. Hocart and W.H.R. Rivers in Island Melanesia, 1908*. Oxford and New York: Berghahn Books.

Jolly, Margaret. 2000. '"*Woman ikat raet long human raet o no?*" Women's rights, human rights and domestic violence in Vanuatu'. In *Human Rights and Gender Politics: Asia-Pacific Perspectives*, ed. Anne-Marie Hilsdon, Martha Macintyre, Vera Mackie and Maila Stivens, pp. 120–42. London and New York: Routledge.

Jourdan, Christine. 2007. 'Linguistic paths to urban self in postcolonial Solomon Islands'. In *Consequences of Contact: Language Ideologies and Sociocultural Transformations in Pacific Societies*, ed. Miki Makihara and Bambi Schieffelin, pp. 30–48. Oxford: Oxford University Press. doi.org/10.1093/acprof:oso/9780195324983.003.0002.

——. 1995. 'Stepping-stones to national consciousness: The Solomon Islands case'. In *Nation-Making: Emergent Identities in Postcolonial Melanesia*, ed. Robert Foster, pp. 127–50. Ann Arbor: University of Michigan Press.

Kelly, Janette, Joanne Daiwo and Viola Malasa. 2011. 'Funds of knowledge: Developing a diploma in teaching in early childhood education in the Solomon Islands'. *Waikato Journal of Education* 16(2): 71–83. doi.org/10.15663/wje.v16i2.52.

Langmore, Diane. 1989. 'The object lesson of a civilised, Christian home'. In *Family and Gender in the Pacific: Domestic Contradictions and the Colonial Impact*, ed. Margaret Jolly and Martha Macintyre, pp. 84–94. Cambridge: Cambridge University Press. doi.org/10.1017/CBO9781139084864.005.

LiPuma, Edward. 2000. *Encompassing Others: The Magic of Modernity in Melanesia*. Ann Arbor: University of Michigan Press.

Macintyre, Martha. 2011. 'Money changes everything: Papua New Guinean women in the modern economy'. In *Managing Modernity in the Western Pacific*, ed. Mary Patterson and Martha Macintyre, pp. 90–120. St Lucia: University of Queensland Press.

——. 2000. '"Hear us, women of Papua New Guinea!" Melanesian women and human rights'. In *Human Rights and Gender Politics: Asia-Pacific Perspectives*, ed. Anne-Marie Hilsdon, Martha Macintyre, Vera Mackie and Maila Stivens, pp. 147–71. London and New York: Routledge.

Makini, Jully. 1989. 'A YWCA kindergarten in the Solomon Islands'. Summary of a presentation given at the workshop, Women, Development and Empowerment: A Pacific Feminist Perspective, Fiji, March 1987. Online: nzetc.victoria.ac.nz/tm/scholarly/tei-GriWom2-c2-4.html (accessed 17 August 2016).

McDougall, Debra. 2016. *Engaging with Strangers: Love and Violence in the Rural Solomon Islands*. ASAO Studies in Pacific Anthropology, vol. 6. New York and Oxford: Berghahn.

——. 2014. '"Tired for nothing": Women, chiefs, and the domestication of customary authority in Solomon Islands'. In *Divine Domesticities: Christian Paradoxes in Asia and the Pacific*, ed. Hyaeweol Choi and Margaret Jolly, pp. 199–224. Canberra: ANU Press. Online: press. anu.edu.au/publications/divine-domesticities (accessed 12 August 2016).

——. 2012. 'Stealing foreign words, recovering local treasures: Bible translation and vernacular literacy on Ranongga (Solomon Islands)'. *The Australian Journal of Anthropology* 23(3): 318–39. doi.org/10.1111/taja.12003.

——. 2003. 'Fellowship and citizenship as models of national community: United Church Women's Fellowship in Ranongga, Solomon Islands'. *Oceania* 74(1–2): 61–80.

McKeown, Eamonn. 2001. 'Biros, books and big-men: Literacy and the transformation of leadership in Simbu, Papua New Guinea'. *Oceania* 72(2): 105–16. doi.org/10.1002/j.1834-4461.2001.tb02775.x.

Merry, Sally Engel. 2003. 'Human rights law and the demonization of culture (and anthropology along the way)'. *Political and Legal Anthropology Review* 26(1): 55–76. doi.org/10.1525/pol.2003.26.1.55.

Ministry of Education and Human Resources Development (MEHRD). 2013. *MEHRD Performance Assessment Report 2006–2013*. Honiara: Ministry of Education and Human Resources Development.

Monson, Rebecca. 2013. 'Vernacularising political participation: Strategies of women peace-builders in Solomon Islands'. *Intersections: Gender and Sexuality in Asia and the Pacific* 33. Online: intersections. anu.edu.au/issue33/monson.htm (accessed 18 June 2016).

Munro, Jenny. 2013. 'The violence of inflated possibilities: Education, transformation and diminishment in Wamena, Papua'. *Indonesia* 95: 25–46. doi.org/10.1353/ind.2013.0008.

Pollard, Alice Aruhe'eta. 2003. 'Women's organizations, voluntarism, and self-financing in Solomon Islands: A participant perspective'. *Oceania* 74(1–2): 44–60.

———. 2000. *Givers of Wisdom, Labourers Without Gain: Essays on Women in Solomon Islands*, ed. Anthony Walker. Suva: Institute of Pacific Studies, University of the South Pacific.

Rousseau, Benedicta. 2008. '"This is a court of law, not a court of morality": *Kastom* and custom in Vanuatu state courts'. *Journal of South Pacific Law* 12(2): 15–27.

Sahlins, Marshall. 1992. 'The economics of develop-man in the Pacific'. *Res* 21: 12–25. doi.org/10.1086/resv21n1ms20166839.

Scheyvens, Regina. 2003. 'Church women's groups and the empowerment of women in Solomon Islands'. *Oceania* 74(1–2): 24–43. doi. org/10.1002/j.1834-4461.2003.tb02834.x.

Sharp, Timothy, John Cox, Ceridwen Spark, Stephanie Lusby and Michelle Rooney. 2015. 'The formal, the informal and the precarious: making a living in urban Papua New Guinea'. State Society and Governance in Melanesia, discussion paper 2015/2. Canberra: The Australian National University.

Spark, Ceridwen. 2011. 'Gender trouble in town: Educated women eluding male domination, gender violence and marriage in Papua New Guinea'. *The Asia-Pacific Journal of Anthropology* 12(2): 164–79. doi.or g/10.1080/14442213.2010.546425.

Strachan, Jane. 2009. 'Women and educational leadership in New Zealand and Melanesia'. In *Women Leading Education Across the Continents: Sharing the Spirit, Fanning the Flame*, ed. Helen Sobehart, pp. 100–109. Lanham, MA: Rowman and Littlefield Education.

Taylor, Charles. 2004. *Modern Social Imaginaries*. Durham, NC: Duke University Press.

Taylor, John. 2008. 'The social life of rights: "Gender antagonism", modernity and *raet* in Vanuatu'. *The Australian Journal of Anthropology* 19(2): 165–78. doi.org/10.1111/j.1835-9310.2008.tb00120.x.

Tepahae, Philip. 1997. 'Chiefly power in Southern Vanuatu'. State, Society and Governance in Melanesia, discussion paper 1997/9. Canberra: The Australian National University.

Wardlow, Holly. 2006. 'All's fair when love is war: Romantic passion and companionate marriage among the Huli of Papua New Guinea'. In *Modern Loves: The Anthropology of Romantic Courtship and Companionate Marriage*, ed. Jennifer Hirsch and Holly Wardlow, pp. 51–77. Ann Arbor: University of Michigan Press.

Watson-Gegeo, Karen and David Gegeo. 1991. 'The impact of church affiliation on language use in Kwara'ae (Solomon Islands)'. *Language in Society* 20: 533–55. doi.org/10.1017/S0047404500016717.

Young, Michael. 1989. 'Suffer the children: Wesleyans in the D'Entrecasteux'. In *Family and Gender in the Pacific: Domestic Contradictions and the Colonial Impact*, ed. Margaret Jolly and Martha Macintyre, pp. 108–35. Cambridge: Cambridge University Press. doi.org/10.1017/CBO9781139084864.007.

4

Casting her vote: Women's political participation in Solomon Islands

Pauline Soaki

University of Melbourne

Women's political participation is recognised as a major factor in attaining gender equality in developing nations. In one of the reports on the Millennium Development Goals it is stated that 'Development policies and actions that fail to take gender inequality into account and fail to address disparities between males and females will have limited effectiveness and serious cost implications' (Birdsall, Ibrahim and Rao 2004: iv). In Solomon Islands, female participation in democratic processes has only recently been seriously considered and the impetus has come mainly from external agencies such as United Nations Development Fund for Women (UNIFEM, now UN Women). International agencies have emphasised participation in government and encouraged women to stand for election. In 2008, the Solomon Islands Government Caucus received a submission from women's groups to introduce reserved seats for women led by the committee for Women In Shared Decision-Making (WISDM). To date nothing has eventuated.

In this chapter, I draw on research with women voters and women who have been candidates in national elections to explore some of the reasons why it is so difficult for women to be elected. I look at some of the ways that women conceptualise voting. Recent scholarly works and reports on women's political participation have mostly concentrated on encouraging women to contest seats in parliament or assemblies, and much less attention has been paid to women's involvement as voters. The studies by Ronald Inglehart and Pippa Norris and other foreign observers (Inglehart and Norris 2000, 2003; Inglehart, Norris and Welzel 2002) on voting behaviour and voters' turnout included women's political participation; and the analyses by Jon Fraenkel (2006) and Jeffrey Steeves (2011) on political behaviour highlight the gaps in research on female voters. Terence Wood's (2012b) study of Solomon Islands elections and his article on the impediments to women's electoral success (2014) stand as the only in-depth examinations of women's political participation in Solomon Islands.

Solomon Islands is an ethnically diverse country, with an estimated population of 515,870 people (National Statistics Office 2009: 22; UNDP 2002) of which 80 per cent live in rural areas, in village settings with subsistence economies (UNDP 2002). The country gained its independence in 1978, inheriting the Westminster political system and institutions from its former coloniser, Britain. Although an independent state, Solomon Islands has retained much of its colonial and missionary heritage, adopting and reaffirming their conservative and patriarchal ideologies. The British administration was exclusively male and established the model of employment in the public service as predominantly masculine. In its encouragement of cash cropping and plantation work, it stressed that such employment was exclusively male (McDougall 2003). While the situation has altered since independence, the view that women should 'stay in the village' and be wives and mothers remains strong. Missionaries stressed the domestic role of Christian mothers, teaching skills in housekeeping, sewing and cooking. In many respects, these colonial attitudes reinforced the male dominance that characterised precolonial society. Today women are citizens in a postcolonial state, but very few consider standing for election and, when they do, they gain little support from women voters.

Solomon Islands has nine provinces, which are politically divided into 50 constituencies, and total 164 political wards (Cox and Morrison 2004). The National Parliament has 50 seats for the Members of Parliament (MPs). The government in office governing with ministerial portfolios form the Cabinet, and MPs without portfolios make up the Caucus. The Honiara City Council has 12 Wards, and the Mayor heads the council. In the provinces, the provincial ward members form the Provincial Government with the Premier as the head. In the 35 years of independence, Solomon Islands has had only one woman occupy a seat in the National Parliament for two terms, from 1989 to 2001 (Commonwealth Secretariat 2010; Dinnen and Firth 2008; Fraenkel 2006; Huffer 2006). In the provincial assemblies, women have fared better—an indication of changes in the perception of women's capacity for political leadership. In 2009, only six women were elected to Provincial Assemblies. For the Western Provincial election, with 26 wards in the province, of the eight women who contested, the only (and first) woman to win a provincial seat was from Ward 14, Kusaghe of North New Georgia. In the following election, Ward 10 Irinqila elected a woman candidate, making her the second woman to win a seat. The first woman unfortunately lost her seat in 2011. Hilda Kari became the first and, until 2012, the only female member of the National Parliament when she successfully contested the 1989 by-election for the North East Guadalcanal seat after it was vacated by Waita Ben Tabusasi (q.v.) when he became Speaker. She was re-elected as member for East Central Guadalcanal in 1994 and 1997. Vika Lusibaea was the second woman to enter the National Parliament through a by-election in 2012, after her husband vacated the North Malaita seat. In the most recent elections in 2014, 49 men and only one woman, Freda Soria Comua, were elected to parliament. The 2014 election results suggest that contesting elections will continue to be very difficult for women.

With growing awareness of gender equality, and support by the Pacific bodies and Pacific states, 26 women together with 427 men contested the 2006 national elections for the 50 seats in parliament. Not one of the women was successful, and neither were 377 of the men aspiring to hold a seat in the eighth parliament. In 2010, a record number of 508 individuals stood for election, surpassing the 453 in 2006. The overwhelming majority were men as the number of women contesting fell from 26 in 2006 to 22. No women candidates were elected to the 2010 parliament (RNZ Pacific 2010; Steeves 1996; McMurray 2012; Wood 2012b). Thus, viewed from an historical perspective, it would seem that women's parliamentary political participation has declined.

There are significant challenges to women's autonomous voting decisions in Solomon Islands that also affect the chances of female candidates. Women are not voting for women, and we need to examine factors that determine the decisions made by women who vote in national and provincial elections. Women in political office or leadership positions can influence other women through their investment in policy and programs for women's issues. They can also change conditions in politics through more conscious, concerted, direct attention to women's concerns. A single woman with a strong party affiliation or high position in political office could contribute to reshaping politics, and lobbying for pushing the agenda for modernisation processes that improve the lives of people. According to John Wells Kingdon and James A. Thurber (1984), these individuals are called policy entrepreneurs. Although there are debates surrounding the feminisation of the position (for example, women in leadership are often put in roles that are more focused on social development or in health and education), it is clear that when placed in particular ministries, women can have an influence (for example, Dame Carol Kidu in Papua New Guinea's parliament). However, it is overly optimistic to expect that pro-women policies are inevitable. Kidu's successor, Delilah Gore, has repudiated proposals for affirmative action and undone some of the excellent reforms Dame Carol introduced. Few Solomon Islands women have been given the opportunity to become policy entrepreneurs, although in recent years the concerted actions of women's organisations, especially during peace negotiations, have shown that when they combine forces, they can achieve goals that benefit all.

Women's organisations are generally regarded as core initiative takers in issues concerning gender and women's development. Globally, the UN and bilateral donor partners have effectively championed the implementation of policies for women's strategic needs and empowerment. In Solomon Islands, women's organisations have been a force for change that has grown tremendously since the crisis experience in 1998–2003. They have increasingly occupied public space, and so created some confidence in women's ability to participate in the public sphere. These actors take on effective leadership initiatives in both the formal and informal sectors while making progress within the broader community (Pollard 2003). According to Francis Fukuyama (2001), such organisations draw and rely on their social capital, the networks essential for efficient knowledge sharing and action through empowerment within formal institutions of the rule of law and rationality. Social capital, he maintains, is less easily created or shaped by policy interventions but can be cultivated by policy entrepreneurs. However, these organisations entail a built-in complexity where it is not clear who is behind a decision and how much of a role conformity plays in its function within the governing state. In most cases, these actors can only act within the political parameters permitted by the state. In the Solomons, while there are indications that women have the capacity to act in the public domain in their own interest, social constraints remain.

Two main structural factors influence the ways that people generally, and women themselves, conceptualise the roles and capacities of women in society. The first is the historical conservatism of a patriarchal structure that endorses *kastom* and traditional norms; and the second is the long-term effect of imperial colonial ideologies that imposed new religious norms and beliefs. The latter reinforced the long tradition of women having lower status in public life. In Solomon Islands, where government has a fairly remote relationship to everyday life, the effect of both these structural forces has been to legitimate surveillance over women's lives while enforcing conformity to both the traditional values and the introduced Christian religiosity. At the same time, women are excluded from public decision-making, defined as 'men's business'.

There is a considerable literature on gender roles and the position of women in Melanesian societies. Bronwen Douglas (2003) characterises the dichotomy between the 'traditional' and 'modern' woman in Solomon Islands and the contrasting approaches to discerning the reality of the women's everyday life. On one side is the romanticisation of the rural setting—of living in a thatched house, cooking on the open fire, eating food gathered or grown, drinking from the stream, bathing in the rivers, and dancing at night—as enticing and utopic. However, on the other side, Douglas (2003) highlights the concerns of John Connell (1984) about women's oppression: subjugated by the patriarchal traditions and cultural norms, victims of physical violence from male relatives, overworked and burdened by domestic chores, and living in almost total submission to their men.

Alice Aruhe'eta Pollard (2000b) and Douglas (2003) maintain that the hegemonic feminist 'ideology of female subordination to men' exaggerates their oppression.[1] Pollard writes:

---

1   For instance, Roger M. Keesing (1985) explains how Kwaio men considered menstruating women polluting, so women would be sent away to live in seclusion. However, these women saw it as voluntary and used this isolation as rest from hard domestic chores and an occasion to socialise with other women.

women do not actually see their role in society as degrading … Solomon Islands woman is proud of herself and her supportive role; she knows that the success of husbands—as of men in general—is simply a reflection of the success of their wives, and of women in general (2000b: 4).

Ratna Kapur (2002) criticises Western emphasis on female subordination, maintaining that such representations of women as victims effectively diminishes their gender status and their capacities to act in their own interests.

However, a further examination of those who present a more positive view of 'traditional' female roles does little to dispel the idea that they are subordinate to men. Pollard (2000a, 2000b) maintains that, traditionally, women were brought up to respect their elders, to be nurturant in their social roles, to be good daughters, good wives, and daughters-in-law and mothers. Douglas (2003) and Christine Dureau (1993) argue that Melanesian women generally are socialised from infancy to be domestic, respectful, and passive. Bruce M. Knauft (1997) and Hilary Charlesworth (2008), with others, acknowledge that Melanesian women are considered the backbone of domestic life but all concede that their contribution to non-domestic decisions is limited or even non-existent. Kenneth Brown and Jennifer Corrin Care (1998) explain that women's status lies in the gendered roles they occupy as child bearers and in domestic labour—roles that do not prepare them for political participation in the public sphere.

The condition and status of women today varies from place to place and reflects their adaptation to the existing socioeconomic structures and the political institutions that define them, with a distinct dichotomy between 'traditional' and 'modern' women. My research revealed some clear distinctions between women in town and those in rural areas.[2] Rural communities have continued to maintain strong attachments to *kastom* and traditional control over women, but the situation is more complicated in urban areas. People from different regions live side by side, and the network of kin relationships is fragmented. But only a small percentage of women, notably those who have benefited from higher education and are familiar with more cosmopolitan ways of life, question their social position and resist the surveillance of their lives in terms of religion and *kastom*. In discussions with women, many indicated that higher education

---

2   Research was conducted with women in White River, Honiara, and women in Kusaghe and Irigilla, Western Province, in June and July 2014.

and experience of travel overseas were desirable qualities in a political candidate; however, they expected such women to conform to behaviours and attitudes that were more parochial and limited.

Brown and Care (1998) maintain that regulation of the customary regime not only maintains male power and control, but the structures and institutions of customary society are dominated by males to the point where women in effect are subtly prohibited from ever having authority over men. Women who were candidates in elections tended to agree with this view. This has implications in employment as well as in political contests. For example, Asenati Liki (2010) insisted that the right to equal opportunity in the work place endorses the right of suitably qualified women to occupy senior positions on the basis of merit; but in practice the assumption of a senior or managerial position by a Solomon Islands woman would be viewed as an inappropriate intrusion into 'big man' public space and status.

It is difficult to escape the view that women should not intrude into the male domain. Marion Ward (1995) reinforces the gendered position with specific advice to the Women's Development Division to investigate income-generating projects, credit schemes and so on, for women engage in—as gender-specific activities. These proposed schemes are quite different from those usually proposed for men and emphasise domestic activities such as sewing clothes and selling cooked food. Unwittingly perhaps, Ruth Liloqula and Alice Aruhe'eta Pollard validate the impression of a subordinate gendered position by attesting to the 'core value of motherliness' (2000: 9) ascribed to Melanesian women, with natural attributes of 'God-given qualities such as love, care, peace' (ibid.). She legitimises women's gendered position through their various contributions and responsibilities in the areas of production, reproduction, family welfare, community work and conflict resolutions, and nation building (Charlesworth 2008; Douglas 2003; Dureau 1993). Writers stress women's agency and capabilities in meeting the basic and practical needs of families, especially in communities. However, Pollard (2003) also highlighted women's unprecedented organised public interventions to help resolve conflict during the ethnic and political crisis afflicting Solomon Islands from 1999–2001. Similarly, many have attested to the value of women's gendered cultural identity and their acceptance of Christian duty as peacemakers (Charlesworth 2008; Pollard 2003; Scheyvens 2003; Webber and Johnson, 2008). Nevertheless, the roles specified reinforce the distinction between the gendered spheres of position and responsibilities, with women consistently represented as 'maternal' and having qualities that are inherently different from those of men. In the Solomons, men view these as precisely the qualities that justify women's exclusion from the political sphere. In short, women can have influence publicly, but this is only valued when it involves actions and attitudes that are consistent with cultural stereotypes of women as gentle, motherly and ameliorative.

Women as voters

A total of 40 women voters were interviewed, 20 from urban communities in Honiara and 20 from the rural community of Irinqila, all of whom had voted in elections at the provincial and national levels. While voting is not compulsory, almost all regarded voting as a moral duty. This view is interesting, mainly because they did not connect this obligation to citizenship—indeed, many did not recognise the word and the others held very limited ideas about what citizenship entailed, confining their answer to notions of obedience to the law. However, when asked to specify how they knew about impending elections, the answers were more revealing. A woman in Gizo replied:

> You know when it's near elections when you get invited to go and eat in some supporter's house or when there is a donation to the local church or school by some intending candidate.

> Someone you've never known to have an interest in you suddenly becomes generous and kind to you, offering financial assistance (translated from Solomon Islands Pidjin, Irinqila participant, Gizo, July 2014).

At White River, in urban Honiara, just over a third of the women mentioned that candidates or their supporters came to their houses and gave them money, telling them who to vote for and how to vote. None had received anything since the election. While in most countries this would be considered bribery, in the Solomons gifts of money and other items to individuals and to communities are so common as to be considered a standard method of campaigning.

The obligation to vote was seen mainly as a Christian duty, often one carried out at the behest of husbands. Very few women had an understanding of the duties or obligations of parliamentarians, of the policies of particular parties, or the names of parliamentarians other than their own elected members at provincial and national level. Ten per cent of the rural women did not recognise the term Member of Parliament, responding to the question only when it was explained as 'big man' (MP) and 'small member' (Provincial Member). Seventy per cent of the urban women knew the names for the Members of Parliament representing their constituency as well as the MP for their places of origin, and because they read newspapers, all could name the Prime Minister and Governor General. Generally, rural women did not know the name of the Governor General or the Prime Minister—only 40 per cent named the Prime Minister and 15 per cent the Governor General. Many did not know how the Prime Minister was elected, or even that he was a Member of Parliament himself. In short, few women had a full understanding of their country's system of government. In spite of this they vote in elections; indeed, voter turnout is usually quite high.

All the women who participated in the study were registered voters and had voted in elections, some on more than two occasions. Their participation is driven by their own motivations but within boundaries of socially determined obligations, defining who they are as persons rather than as citizens. That is, they think of voting as a way of furthering private interests, rather than having a say in the broader, national interest. In some respects, we could say that their reasons are not political at all and have little to do with an embrace of their rights.

They all described their motivations as the moral duty of a good person, often linking the imperatives to Christianity, rather than seeing them in terms of citizenship. Conversations with the women in Ward 14 Kusaghe, a stronghold of the Christian Fellowship Church (CFC), indicated that all the women who were of eligible age voted according to the decree of their religious leader who guides and mandates decisions over politics, economic matters, resource distribution and labour allocation. None of the women could define citizenship and all perceived voting as an activity that was considered virtuous within a Christian framework rather than a secular duty. They perceive their vote as being for their community.

> When its election time, my husband tells me who to vote for, because it's announced at the church gathering, the name of the candidate we must vote for (translated from Solomon Islands Pidjin, Kusaghe participant, 40 years, July 2014).

Many of the women in the research claimed to have some interest in political issues, with 20 per cent of the women in White River and 50 per cent of respondents in Irinqila affirming their concern that politicians had good policies. However, when asked to elaborate they spoke exclusively of the benefits that they hope will flow to their community from the MP or Ward Member. These are conceptualised as personal favours by the elected member rather than duties inherent to the office, as highlighted by John Cox (2009). This is evident from the White River women's responses where 60 per cent said that the member played a 'welfare role', by which they meant assistance in the form of cash handouts. Rural women shared similar views, although the percentage differs. In this context, 33 per cent of women described their MP as having a 'welfare role', namely providing cash to individuals who requested assistance for school fees, funeral and medical costs. Alongside this, 42 per cent of the women stressed the 'development provider' role, by which they meant tangible benefits in the form of a community rest-house, solar panel for lighting, and a school outboard motor.

The subjects of women's rights, democracy and modern ideologies that favour women's political autonomy and independence—ideas that challenge ideologies of *kastom* and the church—held little interest for the women. These were described as foreign concepts, opposed to *kastom* and to the teachings of the church, and women either expressed their reservations about them or were unaware of the terms. According to a woman in Gizo:

> Women who came to talk to us about these women rights, we know them to be separated from their husband, and that is not what we want, we don't want to talk about women's right and have our husband leave us.

> No, I hear some women talking about it but I don't know what it means, but when the older women talk about women's rights, they say that in our *kastom*, it's unacceptable.

> These concepts belong to Honiara; they don't come down to the province and raise awareness of what national government say [about] gender equality and women's rights. The policies and implementation plans of the government are hardly made known to women at provincial and village level (translated from Solomon Islands Pidjin, President Provincial Council of Women, Gizo, July 2014).

Many hold fast to ideas that exclude women from engaging with modernity: to the belief that it is a waste of time and money to educate girls; the view that girls are indispensable in the village because they are more hardworking than boys; the fear that girls may 'play around' and become pregnant or marry outside their communities (with a consequent loss of control over marriage exchanges and bride price payments); or are concerned that girls will enter the Westernised urban world and adopt unacceptable attitudes and behaviours (Billy 2002; Connell 1984). The modernists, who are mainly educated, urban women, stress the emancipating power of human rights discourses in the form of opportunities and equality to participate and occupy public space, and freedom to manoeuvre around restrictive *kastom* boundaries. These sorts of attitudes adversely affected Afu Billy's political career, when she stood for election, with opponents describing her as a 'wayward' daughter, a 'black sheep', and one who was not only educated but was absent from church, and engaged in a questionable marital relationship, and who rarely goes to the villages (Billy 2002).

In interviews, women voters claimed that they applied the same moral judgements to male candidates, emphasising that they valued someone who was a 'good person'—meaning morally upright, a regular churchgoer, law-abiding and kind. When asked if a man who beat his wife was 'good', the majority (60 per cent) said that this would depend upon his reasons for doing so. They believed that a husband had the right to discipline his wife using violence if she had been immoral or in some way been a 'bad wife'. These attitudes draw on customary ideas about male privilege and authority within the family—ideas that underpin more general views about the 'naturalness' of male dominance over women. For example, a study in Solomon Islands on family violence revealed that of the 64 per cent of women aged between 15 and 49 who experienced intimate partner violence, 70 per cent of these women accept and justify their partner's action as his cultural duty to discipline a disobedient wife (World Vision 2009). Given that violence against women is viewed internationally as a major problem in Melanesia, this response reveals that female candidates who campaign against domestic violence as a women's issue might not necessarily gain female support. In fact, many comments about women candidates suggest that they are often subjected to much harsher judgements about their morality and behaviour than their male counterparts (see also Wood 2014: 1).

Women interviewed were unconcerned about the political performance of representatives based on policy development and successful implementation of national strategies. This is mainly because they have no idea about the government's plans and policies. These are available but not easily accessible to the majority of women, many of whom are illiterate or too inhibited to raise questions about such matters, or too burdened with domestic responsibilities to seek out this information.

Although women in the study indicated a willingness to vote for a woman, women who had stood for election believed that there were strong social reasons why women did not do so. In particular, they explained this as resistance to the idea of a woman gaining wealth or power over others:

> Some women are jealous when they see a female candidate contest for election, and this might be because they have past encounters that turned bad, or they think that if that woman wins, she might become wealthy and own things. But such thinking is not levelled at the male candidates (previous female candidate, Central Honiara, June 2014).

> Jealousy is big in our society; women are not working together because they are also competing for positions of employment, in small business activities, and owning materialistic wealth. They don't want to see another woman have easy access to these things (previous female candidate, North New Georgia, July 2014).

> If a woman in Vella wants to contest, no one is going to vote for her because of jealousy; we don't want one of our women to have a higher, prestigious position over us. It would be impossible for the men to accept or vote for a woman in Vella in elections (translated from Solomon Islands Pidjin, participant, Irinqila, July 2014).

> Women are jealous of each other when it comes to supporting someone who might accumulate wealth and power, especially a woman who is known to have unstable marital relationship, or be promiscuous or even have a thriving business (translated from Solomon Islands Pidjin, participant, White River, August 2014).

If the reluctance of women to vote for female candidates because of jealousy is one factor, there are other structural factors that limit their chances of success. Solomon Islands elections use the plurality formula, also known as first-past-the-post (FPTP), for its simplicity. To be elected, a candidate simply needs to have more votes than any opponents. However, even simplicity does not prevent political consequences, which from the outset disadvantages female candidates competing on a 'tilted playing field'. First, they are already hampered by existing social norms and values; and second, the winning candidate does not always get even half of the majority votes—and often gets less. As Terence Wood explains:

> [The] majority of candidates who have stood in Solomon Islands elections since 1980 have won low vote shares, winning less than 10 per cent of the votes cast in their electorates. However, low vote shares are even more pronounced for women candidates (2014a: 2).

Jon Fraenkel's book, *The Manipulation of Custom: From Uprising to Intervention in the Solomon Islands* (2004) and Steeves' article, "Unbounded politics" and the democratic model in Solomon Islands: The 2010 national elections' (2011) offer confronting analyses of Solomon Islands politics. Both authors (and others) share the view that Solomon Islands Members of Parliament since independence were political 'big men' who were recognised primarily for their traditional status and their popularity often derived from their roles in the independence movement (Fraenkel 2004; Fraenkel and Grofman 2005; Steeves 2011; Wood 2012a). Reflecting on the successful careers of men such as Solomon Mamaloni, Sir Peter Kenilorea, Sir Baddley Devesi and Paul Tovua, who were regarded as the fathers of independence, Fraenkel and Bernard Grofman (2005) suggested the recognition of their names has carried weight in the minds of voters. Jack Corbett and Terence Wood (2013) attributed the election of Makira MP David Sitai, whose father had been a leader before independence, and also of North New Georgia MP Dudley Job Tausinga, as an indication of loyal base voters in their constituencies.

However, name alone does not necessarily impress voters, as female candidates who contested the 2006 elections found. Those with recognisable names because of their family connections, or prominence in the feminist movement, in community development initiatives, the church, or those who had prestigious careers—such as Sarah Dyer, Dr Alice Pollard and Afu Billy—were unable to secure seats in parliament, even though they campaigned strongly, promising to bring constituents' concerns and needs to the floor of parliament (Billy 2002; RNZ Pacific 2010; Steeves 2011).

Several scholars have suggested that changes in recent elections reflect patterns of patronage having greater salience in voters' choices than other factors. This patron/client system can be attributed to the establishment of the Rural Constituency Development Fund (RCDF) in 1992, which provided funds directly to the MPs for assistance to their local constituents (Randell 1999). In 1994, the total of the fund was $6 million, allocating $200,000 for each constituency (Randell 1999: 36). Wood (2012a), Fraenkel (2004), Cox (2009) and Steeves (2011) all commented on the fact that new election candidates, mostly men, have deployed gifts and money handouts to the point where political clientelism has emerged as a major factor in successful election. The Commonwealth Secretariat (2010) highlighted this trend whereby voters see the candidates' capacity to provide them with gifts and money prior to an election as more important than their qualifications or ability to engage in national policy formation. Steeves (2011) attributed some results directly to candidates' largesse in the 2010 elections. These scholars conclude that with the political climate becoming more community-development focused, the surprising shift was the fact that a number of political veterans who were contesting for their second or more terms were rejected by their constituents (Fraenkel and Grofman 2005; Steeves 1996). Wood's analysis of the 2014 elections indicates that this pattern of patronage and bribery persists. My own study confirmed the role of payments and gifts, both to individuals and communities, as the major factors that influenced people's judgements about what constituted a good candidate. The provision of services by government is extremely poor and people have low expectations of the state as a provider of health, education, transport and communication infrastructure and services. Often the elected representative's gift of a boat or roofing iron for a communal facility is perceived as 'government' support for a particular community and this suffices as a reason for electoral support.

The disappointing election results in 2006 and 2010 for Solomon Islands' women candidates provided the impetus for the Ministry of Women, Youth, Children and Family Affairs, together with international bodies, to push to make provisions to enable women to have equal opportunity in political participation. Solomon Islands ratified the Convention on the Elimination of All Forms of Discrimination against Women (CEDAW) in 2002, but the government has been slow to develop and implement action plans as directed by provisions made in the convention (Solomon Star 2010; Solomon Islands Government 2014). Article 4 of CEDAW specifically provides for the adoption of 'temporary special measures aimed at accelerating the de facto equality between men and women'. Elise Huffer (2006) and Abby McLeod (2007) interpret the provision as aimed at encouraging countries to adopt affirmative action to redress the imbalance in men's and women's positions in society, including increasing political representation.

Various reports have observed that even with regional commitments and gender policy reforms, with funding for gender awareness projects (Eminent Persons' Group 2004; Huffer 2006; McLeod 2007; Norris 1968) and an emphasis upon training for women candidates, little has changed. Pacific nations continue to have the lowest level of women in parliament in the world (Corbett 2013; Eminent Persons' Group 2004; Huffer 2006; McLeod 2007; Norris 1968) with women only representing

4.1 per cent of parliamentarians in the Pacific, well below the world average of 16 per cent (Fraenkel 2006; Huffer 2006). Statistics from international organisations show that Solomon Islands currently has one female MP, Papua New Guinea has three and Vanuatu has zero. Fraenkel (2006) warns that gender inequality in Pacific parliaments is often not simply a reflection of women's performance in education or their position in the top echelons of the civil service, since they have been advancing strongly in these areas over recent decades, but rather is specific to elected assemblies, which remain largely male-controlled.

Solutions to the problems of female representation and developing policies that respond to the problems and disadvantages that ordinary women face are likely to take some time. It is clear from my study that there is an urgent need for civic education that could raise awareness about the system of government and the responsibilities of parliamentarians. This might contribute to a more critical attitude towards the forms of corruption that prevail and in turn enable female candidates to gain more support. The obstacles that currently impede women's political participation as voters and candidates are a complex mix of conservative attitudes to women's roles, economic disadvantage, low educational attainment and a moral double standard that advantages men. There are social changes required on many fronts to alter the situation for Solomon Islands women and to ensure that they are able to cast their votes independently.

References

Billy, Afu. 2002. 'Fighting for a fair deal in national politics'. *Development Bulletin* 5: 58–61.

Birdsall, Nancy, Amina J. Ibrahim, Gupta Geeta Rao. 2004. 'Task Force 3 Interim Report on Gender Equality', 1 February 2004. New York: Millennium Project. Online: www.unmillenniumproject.org/documents/tf3genderinterim.pdf (accessed 4 July 2016).

Brown, Kenneth and Jennifer Corrin Care. 1998. 'Conflict in Melanesia: Customary law and the rights of women'. *Commonwealth Law Bulletin* 24(3–4): 1334–355. doi.org/10.1080/03050718.1998.9986517.

Charlesworth, Hilary. 2008. 'Are women peaceful? Reflections on the role of women in peace-building'. *Feminist Legal Studies* 16(3): 347–61. doi.org/10.1007/s10691-008-9101-6.

Commonwealth Secretariat. 2010. 'Solomon Islands National Parliamentary Elections 2010'. In *Report of the Commonwealth Observer Group*. London: Commonwealth Secretariat.

Connell, John. 1984. 'Status or subjugation? Women, migration and development in the South Pacific'. In *Women in Migration*. Special Issue: *International Migration Review* 18(4) (Winter): 964–83. doi. org/10.2307/2546068.

Convention on the Elimination of All Forms of Discrimination against Women (CEDAW). 1979. *UN Women*. Online: www.un.org/ womenwatch/daw/cedaw/text/econvention.htm (accessed 11 December 2014).

Corbett, Jack. 2013. '"A calling from God": Politicians and religiosity in the Pacific Islands'. *Global Change, Peace and Security* 25(3): 283–97. doi.org/10.1080/14781158.2013.810616.

Corbett, Jack and Terence Wood. 2013. 'Profiling politicians in Solomon Islands: Professionalisation of a political elite?' *Australian Journal of Political Science* 48(3): 320–34. doi.org/10.1080/10361146.2013. 821100.

Cox, John. 2009. 'Active citizenship or passive clientelism? Accountability and development in Solomon Islands'. *Development in Practice* 19(8): 964–80. doi.org/10.1080/09614520903220784.

Cox, John and Joanne Morrison. 2004. 'Solomon Islands Provincial Governance information paper'. Provincial Government. Canberra: Australian Agency for International Aid.

Dinnen, Sinclair and Stewart Firth. 2008. *Politics and State Building in Solomon Islands*. Canberra: ANU E Press. Online: press.anu.edu. au/publications/politics-and-state-building-solomon-islands (accessed 22 August 2016).

Douglas, Bronwen. 2003. 'Christianity, tradition, and everyday modernity: Towards an anatomy of women's groupings in Melanesia'. *Oceania* 74(1–2): 6–23. doi.org/10.1002/j.1834-4461.2003.tb02833.x.

Dureau, Christine. 1993. 'Nobody asked the mother: Women and maternity on Simbo, Western Solomon Islands'. *Oceania* 64(1): 18–35. doi.org/10.1002/j.1834-4461.1993.tb02445.x.

Eminent Persons' Group. 2004. 'Review of the Pacific Islands Forum'. April. Online: www.iri.edu.ar/publicaciones_iri/anuario/CD%20 Anuario%202005/Asia/47-pacific%20island%20forum-eminent%20 persons%20report%2004.pdf (accessed 23 August 2016).

Fraenkel, Jon. 2006. 'The impact of electoral systems on women's representation in Pacific parliaments'. Report 2. A Report Conducted for the Pacific Islands Forum Secretariat by the Pacific Institute of Advanced Studies in Development & Governance (PIAS-DG). Online: iknowpolitics.org/sites/default/files/report_120and202_-_the_impact_ of_electoral_systems_57_-_106.pdf (accessed 23 August 2016).

——. 2004. *The Manipulation of Custom: From Uprising to Intervention in the Solomon Islands*. Wellington: Victoria University Press.

Fraenkel, Jon and Bernard Grofman. 2005. 'Introduction – Political culture, representation and electoral systems in the Pacific Islands'. *Commonwealth & Comparative Politics* 43(3): 261–75. doi. org/10.1080/14662040500304783.

Fukuyama, Francis. 2001. 'Social capital, civil society and development'. *Third World Quarterly* 22(1): 7–20. doi.org/10.1080/713701144.

Huffer, Elise. 2006. 'Desk review of the factors which enable and constrain the advancement of women's political representation in Forum Island countries'. Report. Pacific Islands Forum Secretariat (PIFS). Online: www.forumsec.org/resources/uploads/attachments/ documents/report_1_-_a_desk_review_of_the_factors_18_-_56. pdf (accessed 23 August 2016).

Inglehart, Ronald and Pippa Norris. 2003. *Rising Tide: Gender Equality and Cultural Change around the World*. Cambridge: Cambridge University Press. doi.org/10.1017/CBO9780511550362.

——. 2000. 'The developmental theory of the gender gap: Women's and men's voting behavior in global perspective'. *International Political Science Review* 21(4): 441–63. doi.org/10.1177/0192512100214007.

Inglehart, Ronald, Pippa Norris and Christian Welzel. 2002. 'Gender equality and democracy'. *Comparative Sociology* 1(3–4): 321–45. doi. org/10.1163/156913302100418628.

Kapur, Ratna. 2002. 'The tragedy of victimization rhetoric: Resurrecting the "native" subject in international/post-colonial feminist legal politics'. *The Harvard Human Rights Journal* 15: 1–37.

Keesing, Roger M. 1985. 'Kwaio women speak: The micropolitics of autobiography in a Solomon Island society'. *American Anthropologist* 87(1): 27–39. doi.org/10.1525/aa.1985.87.1.02a00040.

Kingdon, John Wells and James A. Thurber. 1984. *Agendas, Alternatives, and Public Policies*, vol. 45. Boston: Little, Brown.

Knauft, Bruce M. 1997. 'Gender identity, political economy and modernity in Melanesia and Amazonia'. *Journal of the Royal Anthropological Institute* 3(2): 233–59. doi.org/10.2307/3035018.

Liki, Asenati. 2010. 'Women leaders in Solomon Islands Public Service: A personal and scholarly reflection'. State, Society and Governance in Melanesia, discussion paper 2010/1. Canberra: The Australian National University.

Liloqula, Ruth and Alice Aruhe'eta Pollard. 2000. 'Understanding conflict in Solomon Islands: A practical means to peacemaking'. State, Society and Governance in Melanesia, discussion paper 00/7. Canberra: The Australian National University.

McDougall, Debra. 2003. 'Fellowship and citizenship as models of national community: United Church Women's Fellowship in Ranongga, Solomon Islands'. *Oceania* 74(1–2): 61–80. doi.org/10.1002/j.1834-4461.2003.tb02836.x.

McLeod, Abby. 2007. 'Literature review of leadership models in the Pacific'. State, Society and Governance in Melanesia, research paper. Canberra: The Australian National University.

McMurray, Christine. 2012. 'National elections and women candidates in Solomon Islands: Results from the People's Survey'. In *Centre for Democratic Institutions Policy Papers on Political Governance*, CDI PPS 2012/1, pp. 1–17. Canberra: The Australian National University.

National Statistic Office. (2009). 'Basic tables and census description'. In *Solomon Islands 2009 Population and Housing Census*. Honiara, Solomon Islands: National Statistic Office, Ministry of Finance.

Norris, Ada. 1968. 'Women's political participation in the South Pacific'. *The Annals of the American Academy of Political and Social Science.* 375(1): 96–101. doi.org/10.1177/000271626837500115.

Norris, Pippa and Ronald Inglehart. 2000. 'Cultural barriers to women's leadership: A worldwide comparison'. *International Political Science Association World Congress IPSA 2000*, pp. 1–30. Montreal: International Political Science Association.

Pollard, Alice Aruhe'eta. 2006. 'Painaha: Gender and leadership in 'are'are Society, the South Sea Evangelical Church and Parliamentary Leadership–Solomon Islands'. PhD thesis. Victoria University of Wellington.

Pollard, Alice A. 2003. 'Women's organizations, voluntarism, and self-financing in Solomon Islands: A participant perspective'. *Oceania* 74(1–2): 44–60. doi.org/10.1002/j.1834-4461.2003.tb02835.x.

——. 2000a. 'Resolving conflict in Solomon Islands: The women for peace approach'. *Development Bulletin* 53: 44–46.

——. 2000b. *Givers of Wisdom, Labourers without Gain: Essays on Women in the Solomon Islands,* ed. Anthony R. Walker. Suva: Institute of Pacific Studies, the University of the South Pacific; Honiara: University of the South Pacific Centre.

Randell, Shirley. 1999. 'Towards quality governance in Solomon Islands'. *Department of Provincial Government and Rural Development.* Honiara: SRI Public Sector Reform Pty Ltd.

RNZ Pacific. 2010. 'Lack of money behind the failure of women in Solomon Islands election'. Radio New Zealand Pacific, 10 August. Online: www.radionz.co.nz/international/pacific-news/191929/lack-of-money-behind-the-failure-of-women-in-solomons'-election (accessed 23 August 2016).

Scheyvens, Regina. 2003. 'Church women's groups and the empowerment of women in Solomon Islands'. *Oceania* 74(1–2): 24–43. doi.org/10.1002/j.1834-4461.2003.tb02834.x.

Solomon Islands Government. 2014. Solomon Islands CEDAW Combined Initial, Second and Third Periodic Report 2012 (W. Division, Trans.). Honiara: Ministry of Women, Youth, Children and Family Affairs.

Solomon Star. 2010. 'Solomon Islands Government defies CEDAW agreements: Delma'. *Solomon Star*, 10 July.

Steeves, Jeffrey. 2011. '"Unbounded politics" and the democratic model in Solomon Islands: The 2010 national elections'. *Commonwealth & Comparative Politics* 49(3): 342–58. doi.org/10.1080/14662043.2 011.582733.

——. 1996. 'Unbounded politics in the Solomon Islands: leadership and party alignments'. *Pacific Studies* 19(1): 115–38.

United Nations Development Programme (UNDP). 2002. *Solomon Islands Human Development Report 2002: Building a Nation*, vol. 1, edited by Mark Otter. St Lucia: University of Queensland.

Ward, Marion Wybourn. 1995. *Pacific 2010: Women and Employment in Solomon Islands*. Pacific Policy Papers 16. National Centre for Development Studies, Research School of Pacific and Asian Studies, Canberra: The Australian National University.

Webber, Katherine and Helen Johnson. 2008. 'Women, peace building and political inclusion: A case study from Solomon Islands'. *Hecate* 34(2): 83–99.

Wood, Terence. 2014. 'Why can't women win? Impediments to female electoral success in Solomon Islands'. Discussion paper, Centre for Democratic Institute, Canberra: The Australian National University.

——. 2012a. 'Poor political governance in Solomon Islands – is culture the cause?' 21 August. DevPolicyBlog. *Development Policy Centre*. Online: devpolicy.org/poor-political-governance-in-solomon-islands-what-use-rational-choice-explanations20120821/ (accessed 23 August 2016).

——. 2012b. 'Why voting in Solomons is unlikely to simply be driven by clan identity'. *Waylaid Dialectic*, 29 July. Online: waylaiddialectic. wordpress.com/2012/07/29/why-voting-in-solomons-is-unlikely-to-simply-be-driven-by-clan-identity/ (accessed 23 August 2016).

World Vision. 2009. *Tackling Gender Based Violence in the Solomon Islands*. Online: www.worldvision.com.au/global-issues/work-we-do/poverty/ tackling-gender-based-violence (accessed 23 August 2016).

5

'I won't go hungry if he's not around': 'Working class' urban Melanesian women's agency in intimate relationships

Ceridwen Spark

RMIT University

Introduction

In March 2014, I went to Solomon Islands to interview members of the Young Women's Parliamentary Group. Discussing some of the people who have been an influence on her, Melinda mentioned her aunt. She said spending time with this 'outspoken' woman during her adolescence had taught her that:

> You don't have to wait for a man to buy you a house, you don't have to marry someone who has a job so you can have your future secured, you can secure that for yourself … The culture in the Solomon Islands is that you have to marry someone who has a good job, someone who has land, who has resources and then he can provide for your children but my Aunt taught me otherwise, no, you can do it for yourself. You don't need a man to make your life better (interview, Melinda, aged 30, Honiara, March 2014).

Melinda's perspective is indicative of the increase in status that Melanesian women experience as a result of education and formal employment (Marksbury 1993). Her assertiveness reflects a transformed society in which educated women in Melanesia can choose to focus on work rather than domestic lives, as well as whether or not they want to share these lives with a partner.

Perhaps surprisingly given the strength of her above statements, Melinda has a partner. Describing herself as being in a 'de facto relationship', she was pregnant with her first child when we met. But her description of her relationship, like those described by a number of the other young women I have met, strongly reflects the ideal of gender harmony as emphasised among educated and urban-dwelling Melanesians (see Cox and Macintyre 2014; Hirsch and Wardlow (eds) 2006).

I have written previously about Papua New Guinean women's reluctance to marry their countrymen because they fear doing so will thwart their personal and career ambitions and place them at risk of harassment and violence (Spark 2010, 2011). In this chapter, I consider urban Melanesian women's agency in their intimate relationships. Drawing on interviews with young women in Port Moresby, PNG, and Port Vila, Vanuatu, I explore the perspectives of women who are successfully negotiating intimate partnerships and family life, including in some cases as single mothers (for discussion of other work emerging from this research see Spark and Corbett 2016). This perspective reveals the decreasing significance of kin networks and the increasing influence of individualism and ideas of gender equity and personal fulfilment on attitudes to marriage. Adding to the developing body of knowledge about urban women in Melanesia (Cummings 2008, 2013a, 2013b; Hukula 2012; Macintyre 2011; Rosi and Zimmer-Tamakoshi 1993; Zimmer-Tamakoshi 1993a, 1993b, 1998, 2012), in this chapter I illustrate how women's education and employment enables them to exercise new-found decision-making power with regard to their intimate relationships. I also show how their social connections with one another and ongoing support from their families of origin are allowing them new forms of urban belonging that unsettle both masculine domination of these spaces and traditional constructions of gender.

The emphasis in this paper is on educated urban women and space is critical in conditioning their social experience. To that end, I begin by considering how living in town facilitates young women's agency in intimate relationships. I then introduce the research participants and discuss the interview material demonstrating how financial autonomy, social support and support from families of origin enable women's ability to negotiate intimate relationships based on the companionate ideals of equality and mutual respect.

The politics of place: Gender and belonging in the city

In my previous discussions of Papua New Guinean women's desire to avoid or delay marriage to Papua New Guinean men, I suggested that educated PNG women were enacting a kind of 'encompassed', negative version of agency akin to that displayed by the *pasinja meris* that Holly Wardlow (2006) writes about in *Wayward Women*. Building on the work of others (Jolly 1997; Macintyre 2000, 2008; Zimmer-Tamakoshi 1993a, 1993b, 1998), my rationale for this was that educated urban women were constructed as outsiders in their own societies. Because the benefits associated with modernity—including participation in formal education and the economy—tend to be seen overwhelmingly as masculine entitlements, women who are educated and employed are seen as transgressing their roles and threatening to both men and the 'proper order'. In this view, women's presence in urban areas can be read as threatening men's exclusive hold on modernity and the benefits with which it is associated.

Discussing young, unmarried women in Port Vila, Cummings writes that they:

> are considered dangerous not only because they are matter out of place (living in the bright lights of the big city, rather than in the island communities to which they are tied through kinship and *kastom*), but because they are also, figuratively speaking, "matter out of time" (2013a: 387).

Consequently, she says it is not surprising that 'these young women spoke longingly of their futures—futures in which they would marry, have children, and be able to command the respect accorded to mothers' (ibid.). Her insights highlight the inextricable connections between women's sense of belonging in a place and their decisions and desires in relation to marriage and partnership.

My recent conversations with women in Port Moresby suggest that educated urban women feel more at home in the urban centres of Melanesia than they have previously. The increasing prevalence of representations of femininity, such as those portrayed in the PNG magazines, *Stella* and *Lily* (Spark 2014a, 2015), and the ongoing influence of human rights discourses emphasising gender equality, are giving rise to new, more globally focused versions of femininity in which being educated, employed and having the capacity to consume matter more than the familial affiliations and associated productivity created through marriage. Displacing more traditional constructions of femininity, at least among the so-called 'elites' or 'working class' (Cox 2014), these changes would appear to be shifting single urban women's experiences of life in the region's cities and towns. Where once isolation, harassment and embattlement were the norm particularly for single women living in Port Moresby (Johnson 1984), these experiences are now offset by opportunities to enter and enjoy parts of the city without being accompanied by men.

In both Port Moresby and Port Vila, women find support in their friendships with one another, meeting often in the town's safe places such as at the cafés, restaurants and gyms within the large hotels. Since opening in 2011, Vision City, a large enclosed shopping mall in Waigani, Port Moresby, has become a meeting place for women wishing to 'dress up', shop or meet friends in a secure environment (for a discussion of Vision City as a middle-class place, see Barbara, Cox and Leach 2015). Women's choice to meet at such places suggests that these new spaces of commodification are important sites of belonging for educated and employed women, serving as a reminder that 'commodification is not simply a process by which the colonized, the "native", tradition is corrupted' (Jacobs 1996: 161) but also one in which oppressed groups can articulate a new sense of self.

With these more positive or at least ambivalent possibilities in mind, in this chapter I take a more optimistic perspective than I have previously, arguing that some among the educated urban cohort of women I discuss are experiencing positive agency of a kind hitherto unimaginable in Melanesia. Without discounting the ongoing security issues that limit women's mobility and personal freedom in Port Moresby (Spark 2014b), and to a lesser extent Port Vila, I argue that these urban centres are important sites for women to contest and reinvent essentialised constructions of identity and place.

The lives of both the educated urban women I discuss and the rural Huli women insightfully analysed by Wardlow are shaped by what Margaret Jolly calls the 'twin agents of modernity' (2015: 66): the commodity economy and Christian missionisation (see also Taylor and Morgain 2015). In the rural contexts of Melanesia, the kin networks and social systems that have historically supported women have been and continue to be eroded as men leave to pursue wage labour. Whereas educated women in the country's urban centres still lag behind men in terms of their employment in the formal sector (Jolly et al. 2015), they are better placed than their rural counterparts to access the kinds of jobs that bring both money and prestige. Consequently, the key difference between the educated urban women I discuss and rural women in both PNG and Vanuatu relates to the former's financial autonomy and the status this brings. In turn, women's improved socioeconomic status enhances their ability to access the psychosocial resources necessary for mental health and support. Discussing social support among women in rural PNG, Rachael Hinton and Jaya Earnest note that 'distance' plays a part in restricting women's access to support networks. Alongside a 'heavy workload, familial obligations, and a husband's control over his wife's movements', all of which 'restrict a woman's ability to socialize and make social contacts' (2011: 233), women in villages are more likely than their urban counterparts to experience 'distance' because they typically separate from their families of origin and long-term support networks when they marry.

But, as Jolly notes, the desire to construct oneself outside traditional kinship systems is 'not just confined to the urban elite' (2015: 73). Rural women in PNG can and do demonstrate a desire to position themselves outside the marriage system. However, they have varying degrees of success in doing so, with many seeking eventually to reintegrate themselves into their families and communities because of the high price and precarity of their autonomy (Wardlow 2006; see also Jolly et al. 2015). Discussing the 'passenger women' who seek to get back 'inside the fence' of kin-based systems of belonging, Wardlow writes:

> All of them chafed under the restrictions they had decided to reimpose upon themselves, but all of them wanted to relinquish their former way of life for the security of being known as a *wali ore* (good or proper woman) (Wardlow 2006: 223).

Educated and employed women living in the urban centres of Port Moresby and Port Vila are aware that they inhabit Christian communities and are not immune from the criticism to which they can be subject when they make unconventional choices about relationships and family. But, arguably, unlike the passenger women Wardlow discusses, young women's security in an urban community is beginning to depend less on their reputations than on their capacity to support themselves financially. Moreover, whereas 'wayward women' are unable to exert much influence on their kin—indeed disappointment with the kinship systems that once supported women is a factor in their decision to engage in transactional sex—educated urban women wield forms of power historically associated with men because they earn and share money with their families, enhancing their status and decision-making power (see Gewertz and Errington 1999; Hukula 2012; Koczberski 2002; Sharp et al. 2015). Prioritising personal independence and mutually respectful relationships over church- or custom-defined ideas about what makes a 'good woman', many are accruing the benefits of self-propriety whether they are married, have children or not. Indeed, it would appear that in urban centres, ideas about what makes a good woman are now starting to echo those about what makes a good man—namely, someone who supports their family and helps to steer those with limited education. Consequently, in the cities of Port Vila and Port Moresby, the experience of belonging thus seems to be becoming less about gender and marital status than the capacity to earn money. This belonging is circumscribed by security challenges, but security is also mediated by income, including, most significantly, whether or not women can afford a car, an objective that was a high priority among those I spoke with, especially in Port Moresby.

Professional urban women's financial autonomy marks them as different from the majority of their counterparts for whom marriage is still the pathway to social belonging and protection, including in urban areas. Discussing Vanuatu, Maggie Cummings writes that 'often, married women bring home the bacon, fry it in the pan, and play the role of docile, respectful wife, as well' (2013a: 387). While this remains true for many urban women in Port Moresby and Port Vila, there are an increasing number of women who are more likely to bring home the bacon and give it to someone else to fry. Or, as I am investigating in another paper, to leave home and go out to eat at one of the increasing number of venues on offer in these rapidly transforming urban centres. In what follows, I explore young Melanesian women's perspectives, highlighting three factors that are enabling them to attain the kinds of relationships they seek. These are: having money, peer support and family support. Before doing so, it is necessary to discuss the research method and participants.

Research participants and method

This chapter draws on interviews with young, tertiary-educated and employed women in Port Moresby, Papua New Guinea, and Port Vila in Vanuatu. Not long ago, this two-country approach would have been decried on the basis that it collapses contexts and cultures. However, the forces that have restructured life and the institution of marriage in the Oceanic region have given rise to pan-Pacific revisions of male–female partnerships that make it fitting to discuss these two contexts in parallel (Marksbury 1993).

Across the two countries, I interviewed 52 women. Participants were between the ages of 20 and 35 years at the time of interview with the majority being in their late 20s or early 30s. Most had grown up in urban areas and the majority had completed at least one undergraduate degree, with some having also completed postgraduate studies. In the case of some of the Papua New Guinean women discussed here, I had, at the time of writing, interviewed them twice, once in 2007 and again in 2011.[1] All the Vanuatu interviews took place in May 2014. Those who took part reside in the urban capitals of their respective countries and were employed at the time of interview, the majority in professional roles reflecting their tertiary qualifications.

The interviews were semi-structured and designed to provide insight into the women's perceptions and experiences, including how they view the impact of their familial, educational and career backgrounds on their lives and choices. Although my research was not focused on intimate relationships *per se*, women discussed their home lives as part of a broader consideration of women's changing roles and the challenges of juggling work and family. The quotations used are illustrative rather than exhaustive and have been selected on the basis of their 'typicality' and capacity to illuminate the perspective of this cohort on the subject of marriage and partnership. I have used pseudonyms to ensure anonymity.

---

1   Since this time, I have also conducted focus groups with some of the original participants from Port Moresby. I draw on these focus group discussions in forthcoming publications.

The importance of financial autonomy

Previous research on attitudes to intimate relationships in Melanesia has noted profound differences between the sexes. For example, Pamela Rosi and Laura Zimmer-Tamakoshi (1993: 184) illustrate important gender differences with regard to perceptions about educated urban women's roles. While male students wanted women to be homemakers, female students were studying to achieve professional success and 'wanted husbands who would support their careers'. Other research conducted in the 1980s and 1990s reveals significant differences by sex in relation to reasons for marriage. For instance, women rated 'love' more highly than males while males rated the family, the line and the clan higher than females (Conway 1990: 64). Though not focused on marriage, Jenkins and Alpers' article about youth sexuality and urbanisation notes that young women voice their desire for their boyfriends in 'terms similar to those found elsewhere', noting that, conversely, 'young men, however, seem to have no vocabulary of love, no way to talk about their deeper feelings except in terms of sexual pleasure, i.e. "kisim piling"' (1996: 249). Summarising the differences between men and women, Rosi and Zimmer-Tamakoshi write:

> On the whole, women wanted more supportive, egalitarian, and Westernized relationships while men expected more submissiveness out of their educated wives than was usually the case. This dissonance is matched by an increasing number of educated Papua New Guinean women who choose to marry non-Papua New Guinean husbands … or to engage in de facto relationships that do not bind the woman into a desperate marital situation (1993: 207–208).

These gender differences led Martha Ward to conclude that these are 'nowhere … more pronounced than in Melanesia' (1993: 249).

More recently, John Cox and Martha Macintyre have discussed the influence of Christianity and 'cosmopolitanism' on constructions of masculinity, noting 'glimpses of a masculinity that seeks to be humble, considerate, and loving to women' (2014: 154). Elsewhere, Fiona Hukula argues that constructions of 'maleness' and 'femaleness' in Port Moresby are changing as a result of broader social changes and in and through men's and women's relationships with one another (2012: 90). She writes:

In addition to the changing roles of women, new ideas of being a man complement and challenge the old ideas of maleness. NGO campaigns advocating for the eradication of violence against women portray the non-violent unaggressive man as the ideal type. Priests and pastors who urge their congregations to adhere to Christian principles of love and respect also espouse similar notions and ideals from the pulpit (ibid.: 154).

While most of the women I spoke to identify as Christian, several indicated that they no longer attend church. A minority even suggested (somewhat sheepishly) that their Christianity was more a remnant influence from their childhoods than an active and ongoing part of their lives. Nevertheless, whether they were strong, practising Christians or not, among this cohort, there is a general consensus that Christianity promotes gender equity rather than female subordination (Hermkens 2012). As Susan put it, 'I want them [men] to know that God created us equal and there's no preference that man should take the upper hand' (interview, Susan, aged 22, Port Moresby, December 2007). Moreover, in situations where women had experienced difficulties in an intimate relationship, none expressed misgivings about not remaining in the relationship on the basis that they perceived this to be their Christian duty. Rather, they were more likely to construct their partners as having failed in their Christian duties if they had been unfaithful, tended to drink too much or be violent. This indicates how Christianity, as a 'venerable set of social norms that include assemblages of Christian and neotraditional practices and ideals' (Cox, this volume), is informing the modern perspectives of women in this cohort.

Below I discuss Melissa's experience to demonstrate that employed urban women are increasingly realising their goal of creating egalitarian, considerate relationships with (reconstructed) Papua New Guinean men.

When we met in 2007, Melissa was 26 and the single mother of a three-year-old girl. She had left a violent relationship with the child's father and said while she knew nice Papua New Guinean men, she wanted to marry someone from overseas. When I interviewed her again in 2011, Melissa was in a relationship with Jonah, a Papua New Guinean man with whom she'd had a second daughter. Though Melissa had initially had concerns about whether Jonah would care for her first daughter who was not his biological child, she had found him to be consistently supportive and loving to both herself and their children. Both Macintyre (2011) and Jolly (2015) have noted that 'money changes everything'.

In Melissa's case, this is amply true, but as the following demonstrates, moving back to the city and away from her partner and his family in the village also helped.

When she became pregnant to her first partner, Melissa was a student. Lacking the resources to remain in town, the couple went to live in her partner's village. In the village, Melissa was subject to poverty, exhausting amounts of work, violence and the judgement of her partner's family who she said valued her only for domestic labour. In 2007, she described her situation:

> I was the only one working and when I was working, it all went on diapers and diapers are very expensive and food and that's it … My ex-boyfriend then, my ex-partner he wasn't working so it was all on me to be a super woman and do everything. It came to a point where I didn't have the bus fare for the next day and I didn't have lunch. I'd only have breakfast … come back and have only one meal at like 7:00 at night. So I lost so much weight (interview, Melissa, aged 26, Port Moresby, December 2007).

In addition to paying for the food, Melissa cooked for between 10 and 20 people each night. Her experience demonstrates that women's participation in wage labour does not on its own guarantee their increased status.

Melissa's move back into town and separation from her partner and his family gave her the freedom to commence a new relationship with Jonah, one based on reciprocity rather than reliance. Melissa also found a new job working for a large multinational. As part of her employment, Melissa was about to take part in a three-month training program in Australia while Jonah assumed responsibility for their daughters in PNG. In contrast to her previous partner who broke her arm when she was late home from work (see Spark 2011), Melissa told Jonah when she was going out 'for a drink with the girls' and he took care of their children. She noted that this was unusual, saying, 'A typical PNG man would be like, "Where do you think you're going? Stay at home, look after your kids"'. Emphasising that their relationship began as a friendship and that Jonah was 'so caring and understanding' Melissa said:

> To this date, I'm just really really happy. It's like wow, y'know and I'm so happy too. I mean we have our challenges. What relationship doesn't? But when I sit down and put things into perspective, it's like there are men 10 times worse than he is. I've been through with someone who's been at the opposite end, who treated me like, violent and all that, so he's

never even touched me, y'know the most is maybe shout but that's about it. But I'm the one who's ruling him half the time so (laughs)! And I'm so happy (interview, Melissa, aged 30, Port Moresby, 2011).

In addition to demonstrating how Melissa's financial independence enabled her to negotiate a more equitable relationship, her experiences with Jonah are testament to the changing views of men, some of whom appear to be embracing their roles as emotionally supportive partners and fathers.

Elizabeth, a 33-year-old ni-Vanuatu woman, also described being in a relationship characterised by her husband's support of her career and willingness , to share domestic labour and childcare responsibilities. Elizabeth works in a demanding role at an international organisation in Port Vila and said her husband frequently takes care of their children, makes dinner and drops her at the airport when she leaves for work-related travel. In addition, he was the primary carer for their children when she completed her Master's degree overseas. Partner support for women to pursue tertiary studies overseas also appears to be becoming more common among educated urban couples. While writing this paper, I received an email from a 26-year-old Papua New Guinean woman studying in Australia. She wrote:

> You know how I was telling you about my friend Ruth, well, she is here studying and her husband is back home in PNG taking care of their two kids. Anyway when I first met her I thought she was very lucky to have a husband who allowed her to come study here for two years. So in my bias [sic] thinking, I thought hers is one of those rare cases (you know to have an understanding PNG husband). Then I just remembered another friend of Ruth's who just completed her masters in Hawai'i and her husband stayed back in PNG with their daughter too. And while I was on the bus getting here, I saw on FB [Facebook] my older cousin posting about how her husband is taking care of their three kids while she is working somewhere in Hagen. So yeah just thinking PNG men (some of them) must be progressing (still slow but at least they are moving) (personal correspondence, Bernadette, May 2015).

When I met her, Elizabeth testified that this seemingly extraordinary reversal of gender roles is becoming increasingly common among her peers and co-workers:

> More and more, me and the sort of people that I work with and people that I know and that I'm friends with and of us women who actually earn more than our husbands at the moment, we are the breadwinners. Not to say that our husbands don't work. If my husband didn't work I'd break his head! I earn maybe two or three times more than my husband. I definitely am the breadwinner in the house (interview, Elizabeth, aged 33, Port Vila, May 2014).

Elizabeth later added that if her husband were 'jealous' and she were a 'battered wife', she 'probably wouldn't feel that I need him around'. Her statement explicitly links earning capacity with the kinds of relationships employed urban women are able to negotiate—and to terminate. Ruby's story is illustrative in this regard.

At the age of 21, Ruby, now a 34-year-old woman who lives in Port Vila, became pregnant outside marriage to a man who offered no financial or emotional support to either her or their son. Her partner was also unfaithful and controlling, making her work and home life difficult by constantly harassing her. When I spoke with her in 2014, she described this time:

> I was really like a prisoner … 'cause he wasn't allowing me to go anywhere even during functions or anything he would be like a security watching me. I wasn't feeling comfortable. At one time I remember he tore my clothes in front of my family and everyone in the same neighbourhood. He was really destroying my life (interview, Ruby, aged 34, Port Vila, May 2014).

After three years of enduring this burdensome relationship, Ruby summoned the courage to end it. Commenting on this decision, she said:

> The thing that made me strong is that I've got a job. I've got security there. I can do anything cause I have good money. I won't go hungry if he's not around, cause I feed him as well so I think that's what made me strong (interview, Ruby, aged 34, Port Vila, May 2014).

Having separated from this partner, Ruby commenced a new relationship with her current partner who supports her career and with whom she shares domestic duties. She described him as 'very, very supportive and trusting', saying, 'he gives me freedom. Anywhere I want to go I just go'. Ruby also stressed the importance of maintaining equity in relation to domestic duties and childcare. She now has a second child with her new partner and they share housekeeping duties and care for their two children, something that Ruby emphasised is important for her children to witness.

When her son came home from school having been told by the teacher that his father was the 'head of the household', Ruby explained that this was not the case, saying, 'Dad and I both work together in managing the house. If you think I can wash the plate … Dad can wash the plate'. She said that because of her commitment to teaching her children about equity in the home, it will be 'a lucky woman who marries [her] son' (interview, Ruby, aged 34, Port Vila, May 2014).

Melissa, Elizabeth and Ruby's experiences demonstrate that having money makes a difference to women's capacity to negotiate intimate relationships based on respect and equality. In the following section, I discuss another factor that is enabling educated and employed women's relationship choices: namely, the provision of peer support in which the expectation of respect and gender equity in relationships is assumed.

The importance of social networks and peer support

Research shows that 'people who have more resources … including social networks, and social support are better able to avoid risk and adopt protective strategies where necessary' (Hinton and Earnest 2011: 225). The importance of social networks and support from 'women with similar experience and needs' (ibid.: 233) emerges as a key factor alongside financial autonomy in determining Melanesian women's willingness to challenge or leave partners with whom they have unequal or destructive relationships. Wendy and Mary Jane's experiences are illustrative.

Wendy is a 31-year-old mother of two who was raised by educated parents and grew up in Port Vila. Determined to follow in her father's footsteps and become a lawyer, she experienced significant challenges after becoming pregnant at the age of 20. While trying to juggle her studies alongside the demands of being a single parent, Wendy relied on her family to assist with childcare for her young daughter because the father of her daughter was not committed to the relationship and was violent and abusive.

After having her baby, Wendy commenced a voluntary position at a women's organisation in Port Vila. The role of the women in the organisation in which Wendy works is notable, serving as a powerful example of the ways in which other women can provide significant impetus and support for women to navigate new pathways to wider social change (Kabeer 2011). Discussing her workplace, Wendy said:

> When I came here I found the environment here is different. Because you know how when you have a child, people expect you to be with the father of the child and so when I came here I saw that the staff here they have a totally different view of me. You know it's okay if I have a child but not living with the father, the father is gone off and they encouraged me that 'it's not only you, a lot of women are like that, a lot of young girls are like that'. So that sort of empowered me, it empowered me and so I stayed and volunteered and continued my studies (interview, Wendy, aged 31, Port Vila, May 2014).

The staff's lack of judgement of Wendy is unusual in Melanesia because of the societal expectation that young women will remain chaste until and then raise their children in the context of marriage. Normalising Wendy's perspective—'it's not only you'—the staff offered a different perspective to the dominant societal one in which women who become pregnant outside marriage are judged immoral, despite the fact that the majority of young people have had sex outside marriage (see Buchanan-Awarafu and Maebiru 2008). Their acceptance and support of Wendy gave her the positive social affiliations that help women to rethink abusive relationships. Wendy's experience at the women's organisation contrasts with Esther's experience of being excluded from church business meetings because she'd had a child outside marriage, indicating one reason why some educated professional women, including Esther, no longer attend church.

In the following passage, Wendy links her awareness of her right to punish her partner for his violence with her experiences at the women's organisation. Her emphasis on the 'empowering' support provided by the women at her workplace provides important insight into the ways in which 'chosen communities' can allow women to critique their situations and open up new possibilities and ways of living (Kabeer 1999).

> He was being violent to me but from me working here [the women's organisation] and giving information to him 'you know what you're doing is wrong, and if you think you will continue to mistreat me like that this is what I can do and I will do it if you do not stop your mistreatments'. And so I ended up telling him to get out of my house and then he realised 'oh Wendy is talking. I thought she would just say but she would never do what she said she will do if I mistreat her'. And so the fact that I told

him to go and be with his family and I can manage myself and my children without him got him thinking. For about a month I didn't take a restraining order. I just told him to get out. I've had enough of you and your violence so that was 2012. Since then until this day he's not violent anymore. So I guess from what I know and what I've told him I see that I've gained this respect from him and he assists me with the work, he supports me. Like initially if I was to travel, I would go and leave my children with my relatives but since then he's been more responsible. If my boss tells me to go to an island tomorrow, I can just go without thinking 'who's going to cook my children's food? Who's going to take them to school?' Cause I know that he will do these things (interview, Wendy, aged 31, Port Vila, May 2014).

Wendy's statement, 'I can manage myself and my children without him', echoes Elizabeth's claim that if her partner were violent she wouldn't need him around, and Ruby's statement: 'I won't go hungry if he's not around'. All three reveal urban employed women's capacity to negotiate their relationships from a position of strength.

While this strength derives in part from women's financial autonomy, it is also a result of their support of one another. Arguably, female support of peers is more likely to be found in urban than rural areas because the latter contexts are more likely to be characterised by 'traditional' forms of sociality in which 'concern for marriage alliances, dowries, exchanges and bridewealth' (Marksbury 1993: 20) matters more than peer support. Noting that the male/female antagonism that is characteristic of parts of Melanesia does not imply 'the easy congregation of women', Jolly observes that, conversely, in many places 'the diverse origins of wives precluded any strong sense of shared interest between women' (2003: 135). In the city and when women are earning money, families are less likely to have a stake in maintaining a marriage, thus opening up a space for friends, co-workers and peers to offer their (counter) perspectives. Mary Jane's experience of leaving a violent and abusive relationship confirms the significant role friendship networks play in shaping urban women's perspectives on their relationships.

When we met in Port Moresby in 2007, Mary Jane was 25 years old and engaged to be married to her partner of two years. By 2011, she was single, having been separated from her partner since 2008 because of his violence towards her. After being hit by her partner, Mary Jane told him:

Enough, stop it, leave me alone, move on. I'm not going to stay here, I'm not going to stay in this relationship and you're going to keep doing this to me. Y'know it takes two to work out a good relationship and you need to accept the person for who they are. And if you love them you should be able to trust them and not think that they're going and fooling around behind your back (interview, Mary Jane, aged 29, Port Moresby, May 2011).

Mary Jane's assertiveness reflects her experience as a young professional in Port Moresby, including inhabiting a milieu in which her friends value autonomy over alliance. Describing her friends' reactions to her partner's jealousy and violence, she said:

Even my friends were like 'just gosh, leave him man'. Cos they would call me like 'you coming', y'know my friend, my best friends from school or whatever, I wouldn't go with them, because of him. Like I stayed away from my friends for like a month or two, no contact or nothing, so it was good to have a little bit of my life back, cause I told him, for me personally, my life is not just you and me and your family, no. It's me, my family, my work, my friends, y'know, it's a big circle, it's not just you, me, case closed. That, he didn't accept (interview, Mary Jane, aged 29, Port Moresby, May 2011).

Mary Jane's confident assertion of her identity outside the parameters of marriage and family is akin to those of young women in advanced capitalist societies. Rather than defining herself in relation to her partner she determines her own 'big circle' and defines herself in relation to her family, friends and career. Encapsulating the increasing importance of voluntary associations, networks, contacts and friendships and the declining significance of kin consciousness (Ward 1993) in contemporary Melanesia, she gives voice to a perspective that is increasingly common among young urban women in Melanesia.

Sarah, an articulate 32-year-old single mother of two who lives in Port Vila, also spoke about the importance of support from like-minded women. While some people were critical of her status as a single mother, she gained support from the educated young women with whom she socialised and worked:

And I see these young women; they're very supportive not just in terms of the profession, the work and everything but also personally. How they provide support to each other, I know that quite a few of them are also single mothers and you know just chipping in and seeing how people are doing you get an email or something on Facebook saying 'how are you going and how can we support', so I see a lot more of that cooperation (interview, Sarah, aged 32, Port Vila, May 2014).

In most parts of rural Melanesia it is difficult for 'single mothers' to survive, let alone to form socially supportive networks with one another. As Wardlow (2006) discusses, fraternising with Huli women perceived as 'wayward' can be a risky business in rural Melanesia because of the perception that people who associate with such women are themselves morally dubious. Sarah's identification of young women and single mothers' support of one another thus appears to point toward a new stage in the development of women's sociality in urban Melanesia (see also Douglas 2003).

Alongside their friends, young women's families of origin remain important. Where once women moved across the land, creating 'roads' between hamlets (see Jolly 2015), today, urban Melanesian women are maintaining longer and deeper connections with their families of origin. At the same time, ideas about what makes a family are changing and there are an increasing number of matrifocal families in which women are the head of the household by virtue of their status as providers.

'Single' mothers and single women: The importance of families of origin

The women with whom I spoke who were 'single' mothers were not living alone but in a household with a parent or parents and siblings or other family members who would assist with childcare and domestic duties, typically in exchange for the provision of accommodation and food. Their status as providers, often for a number of family members, appeared to outweigh any more negative perceptions about their status as single mothers, at least among the family members they supported. Again, such arrangements appear to work best in the context of the city where young women can manage the number of people in their household and travel to and from their places of employment more easily. Away from the village, they are also insulated to a degree from those with more conservative opinions about their single status.

Discussing women's access to money through the '*mama lus frut*' scheme in West New Britain, Gina Koczberski observes that the women involved were 'creating a placed-based feminism that emphasizes the continuing importance of the indigenous economy and forms of production and reproduction that support women's traditional power and identity' (2002: 91). The urban women I spoke with are more radical in that their status as educated, waged earners enabled them to challenge existing gender and social roles. While not turning their backs on their natal families, they were privileging their status as daughters, sisters and mothers over their roles as 'wives'.

Many young women expressed gratitude that their mothers and other family members such as siblings made their decision to be 'single' possible. For example, Sarah said:

> I have a lot of support from my mum and I tell her that every day. I think that if she wasn't living with us, it would be so much more different and difficult but the fact that I have her with me means that I am able to do certain things that I would not be able to do if I was on my own (interview, Sarah, aged 32, Port Vila, May 2014).

Esther, also a ni-Vanuatu woman, left her partner and the father of her young daughter because of his excessive drinking. Because she works full-time in a role that requires her to work at nights and on weekends, she needs support to care for her daughter. Like Sarah, Esther relies on her family for childcare. Invoking the idea of a Melanesian 'support system', she constructs her situation as better than it would be if she were not living in Vanuatu.

> So my mum's taking care of her [Esther's daughter] with help from my brothers and my sisters as well … I am very blessed and very thankful I have that support system here whereas if I was anywhere else I don't think I would have that (interview, Esther, aged 30, Port Vila, May 2014).

The support that the women gain from their families has much to do with the kinds of families in which they have been raised. When Melissa, whom I discussed earlier, fled her violent partner she and her daughter went to her mother's house 'to heal'.

As Melissa said, her mother worked in the area of gender education and told her daughters they were valuable and needed to be 'tough' and expected them to partner with 'open-minded' and 'modern' men. Typically, the families of the women with whom I spoke include one or two educated parents who promoted gender equity in their household and in education, supporting their daughters to attend school and university in the hope they would obtain secure, professional jobs. As a result of their beliefs and values as well as their emotional and financial investment, the young women's parents place great value on their daughters, expecting them to marry educated professionals with whom they will have equitable relationships. When this proves not to be the case, they assist their daughters to extricate themselves from violent or abusive relationships, rather than expecting them to remain in these for the sake of propriety. Indeed, as Darlene made clear, it was her ongoing relationship with a violent, controlling man that caused friction within her family of origin precisely because her parents and siblings wanted 'more' for her on the basis of her upbringing and education.

Because of the high cost of living in Port Moresby and Port Vila, many single women share homes with their parents and siblings into their 30s. For example, Meg, a 25-year-old who works for an international organisation in Port Moresby, lives with her parents and six siblings. She says that cohabiting means the burden of costs is shared and that family members can support one another.

> We all share the cost. I think the good thing about us living together is that nobody really shares that burden … like nobody's fortnightly salary is really at stake. Everybody shares in whatever money they have and pretty much for everybody it's light, it's not a burden whereas if we were looking after ourselves, we were looking after our own rent, food, transport that would be a big burden. We are able to shoulder everything together cause everybody is able to pull in together resources like money that we need so that's the good thing like nobody feels like they're burdened (interview, Meg, aged 25, Port Moresby, December 2013).

This confirms Sharp et al.'s finding that families in Port Moresby 'adopt collective strategies for generating income, sharing accommodation and caring for children or elderly relatives' (2015: 11). Like the settlement dwellers Rooney describes (in Sharp et al. 2015), young women pursue 'individual aspirations' while situating themselves 'in the collective security of kin and common identity' (2015: 14).

But even when they tend to get along with their families, young women struggle with being unable to live independently from them because of the high cost of living. Cohabiting with their parents presents difficulties for women when it comes to having relationships with both men and friends, and while young women without cars rely on family members to drive them around, particularly in Port Moresby, this reliance can place a stress on their daily interactions with family members. Discussing this, Jennifer, a 25-year-old who lives in Port Moresby, complained that her parents still treat her like a 16-year-old and that their attempts to restrict her movements caused considerable friction between them. Similarly, Alice, a 32-year-old who lives with her parents and brother in Port Moresby but wants to move out, said: 'I'm not hearing of a lot of 20- or 30-year-old Papua New Guineans who are living on their own and I find that a real concern' (December 2013). Thus while it may be true that 'it is not as individuals that people survive in PNG' (Barber 2010: 95), professional, educated women who are increasingly constructing themselves as individuals with the right to autonomous lives, understandably experience long-term cohabitation with their families of origin as frustrating.

Conclusion

Historically, the majority of Melanesian men have not necessarily echoed educated women's views on gender equality and relationships (Macintyre 2011). The research presented here suggests that this is changing among educated urban Melanesians (Cox and Macintyre 2014). Because educated and employed women need not rely on men for either financial or emotional support, they are freer to negotiate relationships based on equality, mutual respect and companionship. If and when their relationships do not measure up to these ideals, their families, who have themselves invested in the status of these women, affirm their right to pursue independence rather than insisting they remain with abusive or destructive partners for the sake of kinship affiliations. When financial autonomy and family support are augmented by social networks in which women support one another to achieve their individual goals and aspirations with respect to their careers and love lives, there remain few impediments to educated Melanesian women's bargaining power as they determine whether and with whom they will have intimate relationships. As Mary Jane (still happily single) put it when I spoke with her in 2015:

> With all the men that were coming into my life it's, "Ah I actually don't need any of your money. I'm okay I'm fine; I know how to handle myself" (interview, Mary Jane, aged 33, Port Moresby, August, 2015).

But there are new challenges for these women as they negotiate life in the urban centres of Port Vila and Port Moresby. The high cost of living means that salaries are quickly spent, especially when shared with other household members, and also the extended family. While women in this situation are better placed to opt out of inequitable intimate relationships, they may also find it difficult to extricate themselves from their families of origin if and when they wish to do so. But if Melanesian women can find the right man, it is conceivable to argue that companionate marriage has now come to represent not only the best chance of harmonious relationships between the sexes, but also the highest probability of thriving in the economically precarious contexts of urban Melanesia. Given that one of the fundamental tasks of marriage is to organise resources, perhaps salaried women's chances of meeting such men will increase as men realise the benefits of partnering with such women outweigh any perceived threats to masculinity.

References

Barbara, Julien, John Cox and Michael Leach. 2015. 'The emergent middle classes in Timor-Leste and Melanesia: Conceptual issues and developmental significance'. State Society and Governance in Melanesia, discussion paper 2015/4. Canberra: The Australian National University.

Barber, K. 2010. 'Urban households, means of livelihood and village identity in Moresby'. In *Villagers in the City: Melanesian experiences of Port Moresby, Papua New Guinea*, ed. M. Goddard. Wantage: Sean Kingston Publishing.

Barber, Keith. 2003. 'The Bugiau community at Eight-Mile: An urban settlement in Port Moresby, Papua New Guinea'. *Oceania* 73(4): 287–97. doi.org/10.1002/j.1834-4461.2003.tb02825.x.

Buchanan-Awarafu, Holly and Rose Maebiru. 2008. 'Smoke from fire: Desire and secrecy in Auki, Solomon Islands. In *Making Sense of Aids: Culture, Sexuality and Power in Melanesia*, ed. Leslie Butt and Richard Eves, pp. 168–86. Honolulu: University of Hawai'i Press. doi.org/10.21313/hawaii/9780824831936.003.0010.

Conway, Jeanette and Mantovani Ennio. 1990. *Marriage in Melanesia: A Sociological Perspective*. Series No. 15, The Melanesian Institute, POINT, Goroka, Papua New Guinea.

Cox, John. 2014. '"Grassroots", "elites" and the new "working class" of Papua New Guinea'. State, Society and Governance in Melanesia, brief series 6. Canberra: The Australian National University.

Cox, John and Martha Macintyre. 2014. 'Christian marriage, money scams, and Melanesian social imaginaries'. *Oceania* 84(2): 138–57. doi.org/10.1002/ocea.5048.

Cummings, Maggie. 2013a. 'Imagining transnational futures in Vanuatu'. In *A Companion to Diaspora and Transnationalism*, ed. Ato. Quayson and Girish Daswani, pp. 381–96. Chichester: Blackwell Publishing Ltd. doi.org/10.1002/9781118320792.ch22.

——. 2013b. 'Looking good: Island dress in Vanuatu'. *The Contemporary Pacific* 25(1): 33–65. doi.org/10.1353/cp.2013.0007.

——. 2008. 'The trouble with trousers: Gossip, *kastom* and sexual culture in Vanuatu'. In *Making Sense of AIDS: Culture, Sexuality and Power in Melanesia*, ed. Leslie Butt and Richard Eves, pp. 132–49. Honolulu: University of Hawai'i Press.

Douglas, Bronwen. 2003. 'Christianity, tradition and everyday modernity: Towards an anatomy of women's groupings in Melanesia'. *Oceania* 74(1–2): 6–23. doi.org/10.1002/j.1834-4461.2003.tb02833.x.

Gewertz, Deborah B. and Fred K. Errington. 1999. *Emerging Class in Papua New Guinea: The Telling of Difference*. Cambridge: Cambridge University Press. doi.org/10.1017/CBO9780511606120.

Hermkens, Anna-Karina. 2012. 'Becoming Mary: Marian devotion as a solution to gender-based violence in Papua New Guinea'. In *Engendering Violence in Papua New Guinea*, ed. Margaret Jolly, Christine Stewart with Carolyn Brewer, pp. 137–61. Canberra: ANU E Press. Online: press.anu.edu.au/publications/engendering-violence-papua-new-guinea (accessed 12 August 2016).

Hinton, Rachael and Jaya Earnest. 2011. 'Stressors, coping and social support among women in Papua New Guinea'. *Qualitative Health Research* 20(2): 224–38. doi.org/10.1177/1049732309357572.

Hirsch, Jennifer S. and Holly Wardlow (eds). 2006. *Modern Loves: The Anthropology of Romantic Courtship and Companionate Marriage.* Ann Arbor: University of Michigan Press.

Hukula, Fiona. 2012. 'Ideas of maleness and femaleness in a Port Moresby settlement'. *Durham Anthropology Journal* 18(2): 89–96.

Jacobs, Jane M. 1996. *Edge of Empire: Postcolonialism and the City.* London and New York: Routledge.

Jenkins, Carol and Michael Alpers. 1996. 'Urbanization, youth and sexuality: Insights for an AIDS campaign for youth in Papua New Guinea'. *PNG Medical Journal* 39: 248–51.

Johnson, Diane. 1984. 'The government women: Gender and structural contradiction in Papua New Guinea'. PhD thesis, University of Sydney.

Jolly, Margaret. 2015. 'Braed praes in Vanuatu: Beyond the binaries of gifts and commodities'. In *Gender and Person in Oceania*, ed. Anna-Karina Hermkens, John P. Taylor and Rachel Morgain. Special issue: *Oceania* 85(1): 63–78.

——. 2003. 'Epilogue'. In *Women's Groups and Everyday Modernity in Melanesia*, ed. Bronwen Douglas. Special issue: *Oceania* 74(1–2): 134–47.

——. 1997. 'Beyond the horizon? Nationalisms, feminisms, and globalization in the Pacific'. In *Outside Gods: History Making in the Pacific*, ed. Martha Kaplan. Special issue: *Ethnohistory* 52(1): 137–66.

Jolly, Margaret, Helen Lee, Katherine Lepani, Anna Naupa and Michelle Rooney. 2015. *Falling Through the Net: Gender and Social Protection in the Pacific*. New York: UN Women. Online: www.unwomen. org/en/digital-library/publications/2015/9/dps-gender-and-social-protection-in-the-pacific (accessed 12 August 2016).

Kabeer, Naila. 2011. 'Between affiliation and autonomy: Navigating pathways of women's empowerment and gender justice in rural Bangladesh'. *Development and Change* 42(2): 499–528. doi. org/10.1111/j.1467-7660.2011.01703.x.

———. 1999. 'Resources, agency, achievement: Reflections on the measurement of women's empowerment'. *Development and Change* 30(3) (July): 435–64. doi.org/10.1111/1467-7660.00125.

Koczberski, Gina. 2002. 'Pots, plates and tinpis: New income flows and the strengthening of women's gendered identities in Papua New Guinea'. *Development* 45(1): 88–92. doi.org/10.1057/palgrave. development.1110324.

Macintyre, Martha. 2011. 'Money changes everything. Papua New Guinean women in the modern economy'. In *Managing Modernity in the Western Pacific*, ed. Mary Patterson and Martha Macintyre, pp. 90–120. St Lucia: University of Queensland Press.

———. 2008. 'Police and thieves, gunmen and drunks: Problems with men and problems with society in Papua New Guinea'. In *Changing Pacific Mascultinities*, ed. John P. Taylor. Special issue: *The Australian Journal of Anthropology* 19(2): 179–93.

———. 2000. '"Hear us, women of Papua New Guinea": Melanesian women and human rights'. In *Human Rights and Gender Politics: Perspectives on the Asia-Pacific Region*, ed. Anne-Marie Hilsdon, Martha Macintyre, Vera Mackie and Maila Stivens, pp. 147–71. London: Routledge.

Marksbury, Richard A. 1993. 'Marriage in transition in Oceania'. In *The Business of Marriage: Transformations in Oceanic Matrimony*, ed. Richard A. Marksbury, pp. 3–26. Pittsburgh and London: University of Pittsburgh Press.

Rosi, Pamela and Laura Zimmer-Tamakoshi. 1993. 'Love and marriage among the educated elite in Port Moresby'. In *The Business of Marriage: Transformations in Oceanic Matrimony*, ed. Richard A. Marksbury, pp. 175–204. Pittsburgh and London: University of Pittsburgh Press.

Sharp, Timothy, John Cox, Ceridwen Spark, Stephanie Lusby and Michelle Rooney. 2015. 'The formal, the informal and the precarious: Making a living in Urban Papua New Guinea'. State Society and Governance in Melanesia, discussion paper 2015/2. Canberra: The Australian National University.

Spark, Ceridwen. 2015. 'Working out what to wear in Papua New Guinea: The politics of fashion in *Stella*'. *The Contemporary Pacific* 27(1): 39–70. doi.org/10.1353/cp.2015.0019.

——. 2014a. 'An Oceanic revolution? *Stella* and the construction of new femininities in Papua New Guinea and the Pacific'. *The Australian Journal of Anthropology* 25(1): 54–72. doi.org/10.1111/taja.12066.

——. 2014b. 'We only get the daylight hours: Gender, fear and freedom in urban Papua New Guinea'. *Security Challenges* 10(2): 15–32.

——. 2011. 'Gender trouble in town: Educated women eluding male domination, gender violence and marriage in PNG'. *The Asia Pacific Journal of Anthropology* 12(2): 164–80. doi.org/10.1080/14442213.2 010.546425.

——. 2010. 'Changing lives: Understanding the barriers that confront educated women in PNG'. *Australian Feminist Studies* 25(63): 17–30. doi.org/10.1080/08164640903499901.

Spark, Ceridwen and Jack Corbett. 2016. 'Archetypes, agency and action: emerging women leaders' views on political participation in Melanesia'. *International Feminist Journal of Politics* (July): 1–15. Online: dx.doi. org/10.1080/14616742.2016.1189680 (accessed 12 August 2016).

Taylor, John P. and Rachel Morgain. 2015. 'Transforming relations of gender, person and agency in Oceania'. In *Gender and Person in Oceania*, ed. Anna-Karina Hermkens, John P. Taylor and Rachel Morgain. Special issue: *Oceania* 85(1): 1–9.

Ward, Martha. 1993. 'New marriages in the new Pacific'. In *The Business of Marriage: Transformations in Oceanic Matrimony*, ed. Richard A. Marksbury, pp. 254–62. Pittsburgh and London: University of Pittsburgh Press.

Wardlow, Holly. 2006. *Wayward Women: Sexuality and Agency among the Huli*. Berkeley: University of California Press.

Zimmer-Tamakoshi, Laura. 2012. 'Troubled masculinities and gender violence in Melanesia'. In *Engendering Violence in Papua New Guinea*, ed. Margaret Jolly, Christine Stewart with Carolyn Brewer, pp. 73–106. Canberra: ANU E Press. Online: press.anu.edu.au/publications/engendering-violence-papua-new-guinea (accessed 12 August 2016).

——. 1998. 'Women in town in modern Papua New Guinea'. In *Modern Papua New Guinea*, ed. Laura Zimmer-Tamakoshi, pp. 195–210. Philadelphia: Thomas Jefferson University Press.

———. 1993a, 'Nationalism and sexuality in Papua New Guinea'. *Pacific Studies* 16(4): 61–97.

———. 1993b. 'Bachelors, spinsters and *pamuk meris*'. In *The Business of Marriage: Transformations in Oceanic Matrimony*, ed. Richard A. Marksbury, pp. 83–104. Pittsburgh and London: University of Pittsburgh Press.

6

Pacific policy pathways: Young women online and offline

Tait Brimacombe
La Trobe University

In her book *The Network Inside Out*, Annelise Riles (2001) examined the national, regional and international processes that took place between 1994 and 1996 in the lead up to the Fourth World Conference on Women and the production of the Pacific Platform for Action. Nearly 20 years later, the progress made against these gender equality commitments was both celebrated and critiqued at the 12th Triennial Conference of Pacific Women in Rarotonga, 2013. While this event provided an opportunity to reflect on the progress made and future challenges to the promotion of gender equality, it also offered an opportunity to examine current practices of coordination and networking for Pacific women, particularly as a younger generation of emerging women leaders attempted to forge pathways towards engagement in policy spaces.

Scholars such as Naila Kabeer (2011, 2012) and Srilatha Batliwala (2008) have recognised the power of association and collective action for women's movements in their pursuit of transformational change, as well as the more intrinsic impact that this relationship-building and solidarity can have on participants. In this chapter, I explore these themes through an ethnographic case study of the Pacific Young Women's Leadership Alliance (PYWLA), their participation at the 12th Triennial Conference in 2013 and their engagement with both online and offline (face-to-face) communication platforms. It is suggested that recent technological advances throughout the Pacific region have helped generate new regional, international and indeed virtual avenues for participation and dialogue—including through increasingly popular social media platforms. Using the example of the PYWLA, I analyse some of the preliminary ways in which these emerging technologies are being utilised alongside broader, more conventional processes of face-to-face collective action and policy engagement. This chapter is based on data collected as part of a broader, multisited PhD research project over the course of 2013.

Coalitions and collective action

Pacific women face barriers to participation in dialogue and decision-making because of the patriarchal nature of many decision-making institutions and structures, and gendered assumptions about the nature of leadership as an inherently male trait (McLeod 2015; Soaki, this volume). Recent research in the Pacific has tended to concentrate on women's participation in the formal political realm (Corbett and Liki 2015; Donald, Strachan and Tales. 2002; Douglas 2002b; McLeod 2002; Spark and Corbett 2016), with less attention paid to women's participation and leadership in civil society and through the work of coalitions, despite the importance of this domain for challenging and transforming gendered power structures and relations and addressing the obstacles that inhibit women's participation and leadership. Participation in civil society and coalitions provides Pacific women with opportunities to influence the delivery of services and lobby governments regarding issues of concern to them (McLeod 2015).

Civil society organisations and coalitions in the Pacific have given women an opportunity to 'challenge the status quo' in quieter and subtler ways, acting as a vehicle for the pursuit of social and political change and a platform from which to lobby for legislative and policy change (Dickson-Waiko 2003; George 2014; McLeod 2015; Monson 2013; Paina 2000). In particular, faith-based organisations have historically offered women a platform for leadership training and skills, and a forum through which to exert influence (Douglas 2002a; McDougall 2003; Pollard 2003). As such, faith-based organisations have become a vehicle for the development of activist practice, raising the profile of issues warranting legislative and policy attention (Dickson-Waiko 2003).

From a policy perspective, the Pacific region has a strong framework dedicated to the promotion of gender equality—for example, the 2012 Pacific Leaders Gender Equality Declaration to advance progress towards the implementation of Convention on the Elimination of All Forms of Discrimination against Women (CEDAW) commitments, and the Revised Pacific Platform for Action. Women's collective action has been instrumental in the development of these policy platforms, with women's coalitions linking their work to global discourses and key policy agendas to highlight specific issues of concern (George 2009, 2012).

Pacific women identified a particular need to make their presence felt on a regional and international stage in the lead up to the UN Fourth World Conference on Women in Beijing in 1995 (George 2009, 2012; Riles 2001). As part of the pre-conference process for the region, the Beneath Paradise Project (funded by International Women's Development Agency (IWDA) and AusAID) brought together activists from throughout the Pacific region under the catch cry 'See us, hear us, Beijing' with a view to documenting the statements and stories of Pacific women:

> Over the three-year period in the lead-up to the Beijing Conference, this project, involved women from twenty-one NGOs in eight Pacific Island countries. They documented women's life stories, strengths, achievements, needs and struggles through a rich collection of stories, photographs, soundscapes, slideshows, testimonials and poetry (IWDA 2015: 18).

Reflecting on their involvement in these events on the occasion of the twentieth anniversary of the conference and the adoption of the Beijing Declaration and Platform for Action, IWDA emphasised the solidarity and lasting bonds formed in Beijing: 'International meetings provide opportunities for women's organisations to prove their relevance and raise funds, to strengthen networks and create new partnerships, networks and opportunities' (2015: 19).

Scholars such as Kabeer (2011, 2012) have recognised the potentially transformative value of collective learning processes and social relationships developed when women coalesce around a common agenda. Batliwala (2008) suggests that changes in policy and structural norms, such as through CEDAW or the Beijing Platform for Action, could not have been achieved without the collective power exerted through organised lobbying and mobilisation of women's organisations and activists. For Kabeer (2012), this type of collective action enables the formation of safe spaces for women to discuss issues of common concern and facilitate processes of shared reflection. The solidarity gained through building relationships on shared experiences can be instrumental to achieving strategic gains across local, national and international arenas (Kabeer 2011, 2012; Kabeer and Huq

2010). In addition to the instrumental value of such collective action, and the inherent value of coalitions as power in numbers, there are also subtler, yet equally transformative dynamics at play. This is best highlighted by Kabeer and Huq in their discussion of a women's organisation in Bangladesh:

> The bonds of friendship and solidarity between group members had been forged and strengthened through many years of dealing with adversity together. It was the power of these social relationships that they drew on in confronting relationships of power within their community (2010: 86).

As this quote demonstrates, the formation of strong relationships based on solidarity among groups of women with shared experiences can be crucial to the generation of momentum for social change.

Ceridwen Spark (2010, 2014) has described how this notion of solidarity and support is manifest within groups of young, educated Melanesian women. This is particularly relevant given the double disadvantage faced by young women in the Pacific by virtue of both their age and gender—increasingly marginalised from dialogue and decision-making processes that are either male-dominated or restricted to older generations of women leaders. Furthermore, initiatives aimed at encouraging youth participation in the Pacific 'are still dominated by young men while young women continue to face considerable barriers to inclusion' (World YWCA 2011: 13). Even when given spaces to participate, young women face barriers due to cultural and traditional expectations of hierarchy and respect, and a devaluing of their voices by virtue of both their age and gender. Referring to her research with young women leaders in Vanuatu, Spark notes:

> Ideally, young women would derive strength and support from earlier generations of women who have grappled with similar if not equivalent challenges and who might provide a source of advice and advocacy. Unfortunately this is not the case in Vanuatu. Instead, the young women spoke about the collective experience of being dismissed and denigrated by older women … in meetings, emails and in local media … too young to know anything and lacking sufficient life experience to make decisions. The young women were silenced in meetings, or, when they did speak out, berated for being disrespectful (2014: 1–2).

Transgenerational barriers such as these are common throughout the Pacific region, with a lack of formal mentoring avenues or opportunities for information exchange and knowledge sharing. That being said, some examples of best practice are evident through a few initiatives such as the Young Women's Parliamentary Group in Solomon Islands, the Fiji Young

Women's Forum, and the Fiji Women's Rights Movement (FWRM) Emerging Leaders Forum and associated alumni. Despite these initiatives, the collective capacity and potential of young women in the Pacific is not widely understood, with a need for innovative mechanisms to promote meaningful and active participation of young women in dialogue and decision-making.

For Kabeer (2012), collective action and communities of practice, or coalitions, enable women to acquire new knowledge and information, forge new relationships with each other and carve pathways for future engagement. As the above literature demonstrates, this is an ever-present need felt by young women in the Pacific. In this chapter, I draw on the ethnographic case study of the PYWLA to highlight one process by which young women have forged a pathway for themselves into the regional policy arena; and how the Pacific's recent technological revolution has enabled the formation of online networking and dialogue processes alongside more conventional face-to-face participation formats.

The Pacific 'technological revolution'

Until recently, the Pacific region had been relatively slow to respond to the global increase in the uptake of new information communication technologies (ICTs), largely as a result of geographic isolation, small population size, high operating costs and the presence of telecommunications monopolies (PiPP 2012). However, since 2003 the Pacific telecommunications sector has undergone significant reform and deregulation, resulting in lower access costs and increased uptake of ICTs (Cave 2012). In the past two years, infrastructure advances have seen the expansion of the Southern Cross Fibre Optic Cable through Fiji to Tonga and Vanuatu;[1] and the improvement of satellite networks in the Cook Islands, Palau and Federated States of Micronesia (FSM) through partnerships with O3b.[2]

---

1   The Southern Cross Fibre Optic Cable is a trans-Pacific network of telecommunication cables connecting Australia and New Zealand with the USA, with a landing point in Fiji. As part of the Pacific Regional Connectivity Project (funded through the World Bank and the Asian Development Bank) this connection was extended to other Pacific Island countries over the course of 2013 and 2014.

2   O3b Networks Ltd stands to represent the 'other three billion' people who are not connected to fibre optic internet. O3b partner with companies such as Google, HSBC and SES satellites to provide bandwidth via satellite upgrade. Although a relative newcomer to the Pacific, O3b claims that their satellites can offer network speeds comparable with fibre optic.

This 'technological revolution' is being sustained and accelerated by the region's large youth population, with evidence suggesting that Pacific youth are the fastest adopters of new technology (Cave 2012). 'In urban, and increasingly in rural settings Pacific Islanders are using new digital tools to communicate, form online networks and coordinate' (Cave 2012: 1). In 2012, it was estimated that approximately 60 per cent of Pacific Islanders had access to mobile phones (Cave 2012). Although there is a shortage of reliable, more recent statistics, anecdotal evidence suggests that in some Pacific Island countries, mobile phones are at near saturation rate. This widespread access to and use of mobile phones, alongside aforementioned advances in internet infrastructure, opens up the potential for widespread mobile internet access and use.

This, in turn, has facilitated a rise in social media throughout the region. In late 2012, it was estimated that the Pacific had approximately 700,000 Facebook users, with 150,000 of those joining over the course of 2012 (Cave 2012: 7). Five Pacific Island countries were ranked in Facebook's top 20 growth market from April to September 2012 (when considered as a percentage of total population), with the majority of this growth occurring within a 16–34 age bracket (Cave 2012: 7). While more recent statistics for the region are unavailable, it is reasonable to infer that such a high uptake rate in 2012, combined with the aforementioned infrastructure improvements in countries such as Tonga and Vanuatu in 2013 and 2014, would see an acceleration in the number of Facebook users in the region. The unprecedented increase in social media use throughout the Pacific region makes it an under-researched area, with the majority of the limited literature to date focusing on the use of social media and new ICTs for the promotion of democracy, increasing government transparency and accountability and improving electoral processes (Finau et al. 2014; Haley and Zubrinich 2015; Logan 2012); kinship, gender and mobile phone use (Andersen 2013; Lipset 2013; Taylor 2016); and the potential that such mobile technologies bring for increasing the flow of information, finances and transactions between Pacific Islanders at home and in the diaspora community abroad (Lee 2006; Nishitani 2014).

Facebook and other social media sites have enabled the creation of new online communities, facilitated discussion on a host of socio-political topics, and provided Pacific Islanders with new opportunities to engage in low-cost dialogue at a domestic, regional and international level. Vanuatu's 'Yumi Toktok Stret' (over 28,000 members), PNG's Sharp Talk (over 26,000 members), 'Forum Solomon Islands International' (FSII) (over 17,000 members), and 'Fiji's Letters to the Editor Uncensored' (LTEU) (over 17,000 members) all offer examples of the potential of such online forums for promoting debate and dialogue on key issues of policy relevance, as well as broader socio-political topics. Glen Finau et al. (2014) have explored these platforms as models of e-democracy. Vanuatu's 'Yumi Toktok Stret' has been utilised by citizens and politicians alike, facilitating debate between government representatives, the opposition party and constituents, while acting as a source of information and discussion for mainstream media. As explored in previous work, 'Yumi Toktok Stret' has also been used as a forum for debate and dialogue around gender equality, allowing users to mediate competing narratives concerning gender equality, *kastom*, Christianity and human rights (Brimacombe 2016). Similarly, in Solomon Islands' FSII, a popular Facebook group with a mandate of exposing corruption and promoting transparency, is now registered as a civil society organisation in the wake of increasing interest and growth (Finau et al. 2014). The popularity of such discussion groups is fuelled, in part, by increasing youth engagement with social media, particularly in the wake of comparatively few opportunities for participation in more traditional, conventional discussion forums. As Helen Lee notes in her exploration of Tongan discussions forums: 'Young people were given a voice through *KB* [Kava Bowl] and other sites in a way they had not experienced within their own families and communities' (2006: 164).

This increase in social media use has resulted in the emergence of a Pacific 'digital generation' of activists (Cave 2012: 3). Activists are increasingly recognising the potential of the internet and social media as a force for social change and a vehicle for the inclusion of marginalised groups. While these online forms of activists are often dismissed as lacking authentic participation, and labelled as 'slacktivism' (Christensen 2011), such a conceptualisation fails to recognise the potential for online platforms to mobilise movements and collective action, forge new social relations and solidify networks (Gerbaudo 2012; Kahn and Kellner 2004). As Paul Gerbaudo notes, 'Social media have become emotional conduits for reconstructing a sense of togetherness among a spatially dispersed constituency' (2012: 159).

However, these new ICTs are not without their limitations—geographic constraints (with a strong urban bias among Pacific internet users), infrastructure and equipment limitations, access barriers as a result of limited education and literacy, and running costs. In addition, with increased internet access comes community concerns regarding the accessing of pornographic content,[3] cybercrime, fraud (Cox 2014), and cyberbullying and harassment.[4] Online discussion forums and social media have the potential to act as platforms for both progressive and regressive sentiments simultaneously. As noted by Jo Sutton and Scarlet Pollock in their discussion of online activism:

> The speed, immediacy, transparency, global reach, effectiveness, increased means for communication, and potential for civic participation through multi-way communication are only part of the picture. They need to be weighed against the difficulties associated with communication technology—the workload increase, health hazards, costs, techno-cultural shock … and the need to develop new ways of working together that take time and effort to learn (2000: 701).

Pacific Young Women's Leadership Alliance

The PYWLA emerged as part of a 2011 World YWCA process of consultation and workshops in the Pacific, culminating in the development of the YWCA Pacific Regional Young Women's Leadership Strategy (2011–2014). This strategy highlighted the need for a network of organisations in the Pacific to further advocate on issues of young women's leadership, with the PYWLA emerging as a way of continuing such work.[5] PYWLA's goal is to provide a platform for the sharing of information and resources, as well as offering a united voice to hold governments and donors accountable to Pacific young women. In doing so, the PYWLA aims to provide a platform for Pacific young women to engage with and influence policy.

---

3   In February 2015, it was announced on Radio Australia that PNG had the greatest percentage of internet searches for the words 'porn' and 'pornography' via the search engine Google, a revelation that, although widely criticised, ignited public debate about the role of the internet and social media in Pacific societies.

4   Roshika Deo, a candidate in Fiji's 2014 election, whose 'Be the Change' campaign relied heavily on social media platforms, has spoken publicly on the negative comments and threats that were posted on her Facebook page. She was ultimately forced to seek police intervention to combat the cyber-attacks and harassment.

5   Nicole George (2009, 2012) has explored how the local and transnational nature of Fiji's YWCA has historically enabled an entry point for women's organising into a national realm, as part of political debates, as well as playing a central role in regional conferences as a strong voice for the Pacific on an international stage. The PYWLA can be seen as building upon this history.

The model of the PYWLA is loosely based on a constellation model of collaborative social change developed for the Canadian Partnership for Children's Health and Environment (CPCHE), seeking to bring together groups from multiple sectors to work towards a joint outcome in situations where no one group, on its own, has the resources or mandate. This partnership model places emphasis on the role of small action teams, joined together as part of an overall partnership, with a fluid framework of leadership sharing (Surman and Surman 2008). This rotating system of decision-making, authority and resources through constellation partners places emphasis on the natural energy flows present in a group dynamic, and enables flexibility to respond to opportunistic endeavours rather than requiring rigidity in strategic planning: 'constellations are "loosely coupled" together to create a rough and chaotic whole' (ibid.: 27).

Consistent with this model, the PYWLA represents an alliance between a host of local, national, regional and international organisations and networks including International Planned Parenthood Federation (IPPF), IWDA, Commonwealth Youth Programme, Pacific Youth Council, Secretariat of the Pacific Community (SPC), YWCA, FWRM, *Fem*LINKpacific, United Nations Population Fund (UNFPA), UNICEF and UN Women, as well as smaller, grassroots organisations and youth councils operating at a local level. In accordance with the constellation model, there is recognition of the existing commitments and networks of alliance members, with a view to using the PYWLA to further amplify the voices of young women and expand existing connections. The alliance selected FWRM as the secretariat—responsible for the coordination and accountability of constellation members.

Online

One of the first initiatives of the PYWLA was to convene a Pacific Young Women's Dialogue. The first phase of this dialogue took place online, through a closed social media group. Between June and October 2013, over 100 Pacific young women participated in Facebook conversations as part of the PYWLA Online Dialogue Series. Owing to the sensitive and personal nature of these online discussions, and the carefully curated sense of privacy afforded by the closed nature of the Facebook discussion group, the following section will draw upon data that has been made publicly available in the subsequent reporting on these discussions.

The aim for these dialogues was to provide young women with an opportunity to express their opinions and network with each other online, with a view to using the information obtained during these dialogues as part of wider discussions with Pacific governments and the donor community to lobby for support for young women's leadership. Discussion was loosely structured around the World YWCA's (2011) Pacific Young Women's Leadership Strategy, which articulated a desire for young women to feel safe, respected, included, connected and skilled.[6] These five broad themes were leveraged by the PYWLA, with seven specific dialogue discussions focusing on: 1) transformational leadership; 2) sexual and reproductive health rights; 3) participation; 4) bodily security; 5) peer-to-peer learning; 6) women, peace and security; and 7) gender, economic and ecological justice rights. During the discussions, specific questions were posed to online participants, with each discussion being moderated by two people, chosen from the constellation of PYWLA member organisations according to their thematic expertise.

The online discussion began by posing the questions: What does transformation leadership mean to you? What obstacles do young women face, and how can more young women leaders be encouraged? Through these discussions, young women participants identified the characteristics of transformational leaders—particularly inclusivity and involvement in collective decision-making, public visibility, the promotion of social change, and reflection and learning (PYWLA 2013). Participants in the online dialogues felt as though culture and tradition, particularly rigid expectations imposed on young women by virtue of their age and gender, limited their access to resources, information and educational opportunities (PYWLA 2013). These limitations were compounded by a lack of support from older generations of women leaders and limited opportunities for mentoring or information sharing between generations. As a result of this, peer-to-peer learning spaces (such as the online dialogues themselves) emerged as key platforms to promote honest dialogue and reflection, and encourage conversation among peers on potentially sensitive and taboo topics.

---

6   Safe from violence, conflict, disasters and climate change; respected in terms of sexual and reproductive health rights, bodily security, self-esteem and confidence; included as minority groups with recognition of the intersectional discrimination faced by young women with diverse sexual orientations and gender identities and women with disabilities; included in leadership and decision-making processes; connected through a variety of media and communication channels and social movements; and skilled through access to quality education, employment and training.

A strong theme emerging from the online dialogue series was the need for comprehensive sexual health education, and greater recognition of the sexual and reproductive health rights of young women. Participants expressed concern over the high rates of teenage and unplanned pregnancy in the Pacific, with 'blame' for these pregnancies often placed on young women (PYWLA 2013). Participants felt that existing measures to improve access to family planning information and services had not been sufficiently inclusive, with a need for participatory dialogue to break down cultural taboos around sexual health issues (PYWLA 2013). Participants who had engaged with the sexual health curriculum in schools lamented the poor quality and format with which it was delivered, and called for a greater sensitisation of education providers, and greater inclusion of comprehensive sex education, including appropriate content targeted at primary school children (PYWLA 2013).

Despite the diverse sociocultural backgrounds of participants contributing to the online discussion, and contextual differences in thematic issues, some clear commonality emerged between participant experiences. At the end of the online dialogue series, these common themes were summarised into a PYWLA Online Dialogue Issues Series publication, designed as a lobby and advocacy tool for use in the work of the alliance.

Offline

The second phase of the Pacific Young Women's Dialogue took place offline, enabling face-to-face participant interaction. This offline dialogue was designed to coincide with the 12th Triennial Conference of Pacific Women in Rarotonga, 21–24 October 2013 (hereafter the Conference). As such, the dialogue was designed to support the preparation and engagement of young women leaders in the Conference proceedings and associated events by building the practical skills and networks of young women participants, as well as furthering the advocacy agenda through which to lobby decision-makers. Participants for the offline dialogue were selected with a view to promoting inclusivity of marginalised groups, ensuring representation from a variety of Pacific Island countries, and with a preference for participants who had actively taken part in the online dialogues.

From 18–20 October, 26 participants from throughout the Pacific region,[7] came together in Rarotonga for the pre-conference PYWLA dialogue. In addition, nine facilitators were present, selected from PYWLA's member organisations.[8] Over the course of the three-day participatory dialogue, participants developed advocacy skills, identified potential resources and mobilisation points, and highlighted pathways into decision-making roles.

One of the main aims of the PYWLA dialogue was to bring together a critical mass of young women leaders to strengthen their networks and leadership and advocacy skills. As part of this, participants were introduced to the processes, language and terminology of regional events such as the Triennial Conference and familiarised with the 'rules of the game'— what they would need to know in order to meaningfully engage in the Conference. In support of this, PYWLA participants were divided into small groups—known as 'hubs'—to ensure participants were adequately prepared to take full advantage of all advocacy avenues at the Conference, and to provide adequate representation of the PYWLA collective through all conference plenaries, panels and side events. One 'hub' was responsible for the drafting of the PYWLA outcome document and opening statement, as well as acting as a lobbying conduit facilitating interactions between PYWLA participants and relevant delegates and ministries; a second 'hub' was responsible for creative endeavours—developing artwork and interpretative performances for display at the Conference; another 'hub' was responsible for media outputs—curating press releases and managing social media accounts; with a final 'hub' responsible for managing the PYWLA booth at the Conference—ensuring resources and materials were available for dissemination. This 'hub' approach, with leadership responsibilities horizontally dispersed among participants, ensured the collective PYWLA 'voice' was heard across multiple channels during the Conference itself and associated media coverage. As one participant reflected:

---

7   Participants included representatives from Vanuatu, Tuvalu, Cook Islands, Nauru, Marshall Islands, Kiribati, PNG, Solomon Islands, Samoa, Tonga, Niue and Fiji.

8   Facilitators were from Development Alternatives with Women for a New Era (DAWN), *Fem*LINKpacific, FWRM, SPC, UN Women, UNFPA, and Punanga Tauturu Inc. (Cook Islands Women's Counselling Centre), who were the host organisation.

What made a huge difference [at The Triennial] was the three-day dialogue organized by the PYWLA … This dialogue gave us the opportunity to discuss our key issues, share with each other our recommendations … friendships were formed, which would definitely last a lifetime for many … The fact we knew we had each other to turn to during The Triennial, especially for support, sharing of ideas and techniques on lobbying and advocacy, helped us a lot … The young women spoke as one voice (personal correspondence, PYWLA participant from Fiji, 24 October 2013).

The first day of the PYWLA dialogue included a mapping of the regional and global gender processes and key policy commitments, with participants drawing links between work that was carried out 'on the ground' and work being carried out as part of these broader regional and international processes. Participants—as both individuals and in small groups—were encouraged to brainstorm and share what issues they felt were most important to themselves and other young women in their country. These brainstorming endeavours included the mapping of a 'life tapestry' to identify inequality across a woman's lifetime, and the development of a 'problem tree' useful for discussing the underlying structural inequality behind key policy objectives. Over the course of the PYWLA dialogue, participants were encouraged to prioritise these issues, identifying which priority issues could capitalise on existing momentum and link in with particular conference focus areas. These issues were clustered under key PYWLA themes—safe, respected, included, connected and skilled.

Over the course of the three-day dialogue, the young women's priorities were discussed and refined, until they were eventually combined into a cohesive vision and statement for Pacific young women, one that was the subject of mutual agreement and capable of clear articulation during conference proceedings. This outcome document, entitled 'The Future We Want', called upon leaders in the spirit of partnership to respond to young women's needs and concerns. The document also outlined the PYWLA's five strategic recommendations, developed throughout both the online and offline dialogue processes: 1) eliminating sexual and gender based violence; 2) ensuring sexual and reproductive health rights; 3) eliminating all forms of discrimination against persons with disabilities; 4) promoting full and decent employment and economic empowerment for young women; and 5) ensuring full participation of young women at all levels of decision-making. The document concluded by proclaiming 'Pacific Young Women want to be safe, respected, included, connected and skilled'.

The PYWLA dialogue also saw participants engaged in a stakeholder power analysis—a process designed to recognise the different interests and spheres of influence associated with key regional and international stakeholders, as well as identify potential entry points for collaboration on focus issues. For many of the PYWLA participants, the Conference represented a valuable entry point in itself, offering an opportunity to network with representatives from the Women's Machineries in their own country, key international actors such as the UN offices and AusAID, and local and international media outlets. For some PYWLA participants, such networking was often the first opportunity they had been given to meet with representatives from their own national delegation. The potential impact of such connections was not lost on participants, as one participant from Vanuatu reflected:

> I have really used this conference as a way to engage with the delegation from the Vanuatu Department of Women's Affairs. The Director of the Department came up to me wanting to talk about my work, so this has been a great opportunity to network with delegates from my own country (interview, PYWLA participant from Vanuatu, 22 October 2013, Rarotonga).

During the PYWLA dialogue, participants identified strategic entry points for the communication of their young women's agenda at the Conference. As part of this process, space was negotiated for one PYWLA representative to be included in the Conference opening proceedings, delivering a statement alongside the Cook Islands Minister for Women and the Deputy Director General of SPC. Ina Vakaafi, a PYWLA participant from Niue, was chosen. Her statement, drawing heavily on the PYWLA dialogue outcome document, highlighted the value of including Pacific young women in dialogue and decision-making processes, noting that 'no meaningful democracy or sustainable development can occur without involving young women', calling on national governments to include young women's issues on their national agenda.

Some PYWLA participants were able to negotiate presentation spaces in official conference panels—with one participant from the Marshall Islands giving a short presentation on the gendered dimensions of climate change and its impact on youth; and another participant from Fiji presenting on sexual and reproductive health rights and calling for the need for age-appropriate comprehensive sex education. For other PYWLA participants, not included on the Conference agenda as official presenters, there was a need to ensure they took advantage of opportunities for active participation as observers and during question time. During presentations on women's access to health services, one PYWLA participant from Fiji approached the chair and requested space to make a brief statement from the floor—delivering a powerful statement about her experience as a survivor of child sexual abuse. She reflected on the insistence of taboos on the discussion of sex as part of 'Pacific culture' and discussed the resulting lack of sexual understanding she held as a child and young adult. She concluded her presentation by imploring delegates to prioritise comprehensive sex education within the school curriculum.

In addition to participating in formal conference proceedings and plenary discussions, the PYWLA also hosted a side event in the early evening of the Conference's second day. This event took place in the main auditorium and was well attended by representatives from official delegations. The side event began with a creative expression of the key issues facing Pacific young women, including the performance of an illustrative dance focusing on the themes safe, respected, included, connected and skilled. Participants, who had been rehearsing for most of the week, broke into small groups to perform short tableaus, each representing one of the five themes, incorporating sign language articulations for their chosen theme (in recognition of the incorporation of a hearing-impaired woman in the PYWLA delegation). This creative performance was followed by a more formal presentation outlining the purpose of the PYWLA and the hopes that Pacific young women held for the future, concluding with the powerful statement 'our voices need to be heard and urgent action taken … don't forget us, include us'. The presentations closed to a standing ovation from the audience, with the PYWLA side event referenced on multiple occasions during formal conference proceedings and recalled as a memorable highlight for many official delegates in attendance.

Recognition of the value of creative expression was evident throughout the PYWLA dialogue processes, as the following excerpt from my field notes demonstrates:

> When I arrived at the second day of the PYWLA Dialogue, there were five large pieces of white canvas spread out on the ground alongside paints and paintbrushes. At the top of these pieces of canvas were written the terms—Safe, Respected, Included, Connected, Skilled. Over the course of the dialogue participants painted images and words under each of these headings to show how they wanted to be treated and what their hopes and aspirations were for the future (19 October 2013, Rarotonga).

These pieces of canvas were subsequently displayed in the foyer of the Conference auditorium as a powerful visual statement and strategic talking point. This eye-catching artwork was strategically included in the background of many conference photographs and TV interviews.

Throughout the PYWLA dialogue and conference events, efforts were made to include those participants who were not able to attend in person. The Facebook platform, which had played host to the online dialogue series, was utilised once more to ensure that PYWLA members not in attendance were able to have their voices heard as part of the discussions. Updates from the dialogue and conference were shared on the PYWLA Facebook page (both the publicly visible page, and the closed group), and were subsequently shared by participants on their personal pages and the social media pages of their own organisations. During the pre-conference dialogue, these platforms were used to encourage comments and questions from online participants, which were then fed into real-time offline discussions, with Facebook comments and posts attempting to replicate the face-to-face dialogue and discussion topics.

Reflecting on her involvement in the International Forum of the Association of Women's Rights in Development, Kabeer (2012) noted the uplifting and transformational aspects of women's collective action, highlighting the diversity of issues discussed, and efforts made to promote inclusion and respect for difference. Despite this diversity and difference, that 'they can nevertheless come together and gain strength from gatherings of this kind is testimony to the power of a shared and inclusive politics' (Kabeer 2012: 1). These sentiments are reinforced by the PYWLA experience. As one participant from Fiji noted whilst reflecting on her participation in the events:

> Having the Pacific Young Women's Leadership Alliance forum prior to The Triennial is a groundbreaking moment for a lot of young women. It is the first time we have had this many young women present for a meeting such as this … To be in the midst of amazing young women and to hear what they have been doing in their communities and within their networks … is very encouraging and empowering (personal correspondence, PYWLA from Fiji, 24 October 2013).

Throughout conference proceedings, PYWLA representatives were able to present a united front by virtue of the strong relationships and bonds that had been fostered through both the online and offline dialogues. These dialogues enabled a safe space for participants to share their experiences, often at a very personal and emotional level. During the three-day pre-Conference PYWLA program, space was intentionally set aside at the end of each day for honest reflection as part of a 'sharing circle', with participants encouraged to lodge regular 'emotional weather reports' to ensure that they were feeling safe and supported during the emotionally intense discussions. During the PYWLA workshop, participants were asked to reflect and share (either through text, artwork, poetry or whichever form they were most comfortable with) their thoughts on situations in which they had felt powerless in contrast to situations in which they had felt powerful. As part of these processes, many PYWLA participants shared painful personal stories, reflecting on the powerlessness they felt during times of violence, conflict, loss and illness. At the end of the emotional discussions, participants expressed gratitude at the fostering of a safe space for the sharing of these stories, many of which were being expressed for the first time, and the sense of unburdening felt by the shedding of emotional baggage. Participants took solidarity in the fact that they were no longer facing these issues on their own, but were now sharing them with their 'Pacific sisters'. Reflecting at the conclusion of the conference, one PYWLA representative noted:

> Many of the young women were able to articulate their key issues, but were also able to connect with other young women within the Pacific region and connected at a very personal level. During the three days of the Triennial, many of the young women remained connected with each other, and at the same time lobbied for their key issues … The Triennial experience was not only about advocating and lobbying for our issues, but was also about bonding and building new friendships. It was about learning best practices from each other and finding ways of staying connected.

Conclusion

Now, more than two years after the Triennial Conference the question needs to be asked: What now? This is a question that is largely beyond the scope of this chapter to answer. However, it is clear that the role of the PYWLA has changed in the absence of a key regional event around which to mobilise. The number of active alliance organisations has reduced to largely Suva-based groups, with FWRM retaining their role as secretariat. PYWLA updates indicate that the majority of recent events have been limited to Suva-based participants due to logistical and financial limitations, and while regional participants are still encouraged to utilise the Facebook forum, there has been limited structured or meaningful engagement. This suggests that perhaps the PYWLA is losing its broader regional focus. However, as Kabeer (2011) notes, the building of group solidarity is rarely a flawless process, but can nevertheless be an important source of collective strength despite setbacks.

The constellation model, on which the PYWLA is loosely based, emphasises the importance of variations in the natural flow of energy, with the potential for partners to become dormant during periods of low energy or limited opportunities yet reignite to work on a particular issue or activity (Surman and Surman 2008). While it would appear that existing 'natural energy flows' associated with the PYWLA reside in Suva, unsurprisingly given its role as a regional administrative hub, the model would suggest that this does not necessarily result in the permanent narrowing of the network. Perhaps the true test for the PYWLA will come in their ability to reinvigorate in the context of key regional and international events and reactivate dormant alliance partners.

It is unclear what role, if any, the PYWLA will play for Pacific young women in future years, and it is beyond the scope of this chapter to speculate on the long-term impacts of participation in the alliance. Indeed:

> the changes brought about by these group activities do not follow some linear trajectory whereby women go from a state of powerlessness to one of empowerment. What emerges instead is a variety of different processes and critical moments—in the lives of individual women and of their groups—that interact and spark off on each other until they solidify into a coherent movement for change (Kabeer 2012: 3).

Emerging women leaders in the Pacific are forging pathways to policy engagement in a world mediated by new technological opportunities. This examination of young women's online and offline dialogues illustrates some of the ways that young women are able to articulate their concerns and participate in processes that will transform their lives.

References

Andersen, Barbara. 2013. 'Tricks, lies and mobile phones: "Phone friend" stories in Papua New Guinea'. *Culture, Theory and Critique* 54(3): 318–34. doi.org/10.1080/14735784.2013.811886.

Batliwala, Srilatha. 2008. *Changing Their World: Concepts and Practices of Women's Movements*. Toronto: Association for Women's Rights in Development (AWID).

Brimacombe, Tait. 2016. 'Trending trousers: Debating *kastom*, clothing and gender in the Vanuatu mediascape'. *The Asia Pacific Journal of Anthropology* 17(1): 17–33. doi.org/10.1080/14442213.2015.111 6595.

Cave, Danielle. 2012. *Digital Islands: How the Pacific's ICT Revolution is Transforming the Region*. Sydney: Lowy Institute for International Policy.

Christensen, Henrik Serup. 2011. 'Political activities on the Internet: *Slactivism* or political participation by other means?' *First Monday* 16. Online: firstmonday.org/ojs/index.php/fm/article/view/3336 (accessed 13 August 2016). doi.org/10.5210/fm.v16i2.3336.

Corbett, Jack and Asenti Liki. 2015. 'Intersecting identities, divergent views: Interpreting the experiences of women politicians in the Pacific Islands'. *Politics and Gender* 11(2): 320–44. doi.org/10.1017/S1743923X15000057.

Cox, John. 2014. 'Fake money, Bougainville politics and international scammers'. State Society and Governance in Melanesia, in brief, 2014/7. Canberra: The Australian National University.

Dickson-Waiko, Anne. 2003. 'The missing rib: Mobilizing church women for change in Papua New Guinea'. *Oceania* 73(1–2): 98–119. doi.org/10.1002/j.1834-4461.2003.tb02838.x.

Donald, Isabelle, Jane Strachan and Hilda Taleo. 2002. '*Slo slo*: Increasing women's representation in parliament in Vanuatu'. *Development Bulletin* 59: 54–57.

Douglas, Bronwen. 2002a, 'Christian citizens: Women and negotiations of modernity in Vanuatu'. *The Contemporary Pacific* 14(1): 1–38. doi.org/10.1353/cp.2002.0007.

——. 2002b. 'Why religion, race and gender matter in Pacific politics'. *Development Bulletin* 59: 11–14.

Finau, Glen, Acklesh Prasad, Romitesh Kant, Jope Tarai, Sarah Logan, and John Cox. 2014. 'Social Media and e-Democracy in Fiji, Solomon Islands and Vanuatu'. In 20th Americas Conference on Information Systems. Georgia: Association for Information Systems (AIS).

George, Nicole. 2014. 'Promoting women, peace and security in the Pacific Islands: Hot conflict/slow violence'. *Australian Journal of International Affairs* 68(3): 314–32. doi.org/10.1080/10357718.2014.902032.

——. 2012. *Situating Women: Gender Politics and Circumstance in Fiji*. Canberra: ANU E Press. Online: Online: press.anu.edu.au/publications/situating-women (accessed 12 August 2016).

——. 2009. '"Situating" active citizenship: Historical and contemporary perspectives of women's organising in the Pacific'. *Development in Practice* 19(8): 981–96. doi.org/10.1080/09614520903220826.

Gerbaudo, Paul. 2012. *Tweets and the Streets: Social Media and Contemporary Activism*. London: Pluto Press.

Haley, Nicole and Kerry Zubrinich. 2015. 'Mobile phones and the 2014 Solomon Islands National Elections'. State Society and Governance in Melanesia, in brief, 2015/28. Canberra: The Australian National University.

International Women's Development Agency (IWDA). 2015. 'The Beijing Platform For Action: IWDA partner perspectives 20 years on'. *Gender Matters* 6. Online: www.iwda.org.au/resource/journal-gender-matters-6/ (accessed 13 August 2016).

Kabeer, Naila. 2012. 'The power of association: Reflecting on women's collective action as a force for social change'. *Thinkpiece #2*. London: UK Feminista.

——. 2011. 'Between affiliation and autonomy: Navigating pathways of women's empowerment and gender justice in rural Bangladesh'. *Development and Change* 42(2): 499–528. doi.org/10.1111/j.1467-7660.2011.01703.x.

Kabeer, Naila and Lopita Huq. 2010. 'The power of relationships: Love and solidarity in a landless women's organisation in rural Bangladesh'. *IDS Bulletin* 41(2): 79–87. doi.org/10.1111/j.1759-5436.2010.00126.x.

Kahn, Richard and Douglas Kellner. 2004. 'New media and internet activism: from the "Battle of Seattle" to blogging'. *New Media and Society* 6(1): 87–95. doi.org/10.1177/1461444804039908.

Lee, Helen. 2006. 'Debating Language and identity online: Tongans on the net'. In *Native on the Net: Indigenous and Diasporic Peoples in the Virtual Age*, ed. Kyla Landzelius, pp. 257–81. London and New York: Routledge.

Lipset, David. 2013, 'Mobail: Moral ambivalence and the domestication of mobile telephones in peri-urban Papua New Guinea'. *Culture, Theory and Critique* 54(3): 335–54. doi.org/10.1080/14735784.201 3.826501.

Logan, Sarah. 2012. '*Rausim*! Digital politics in Papua New Guinea'. State Society and Governance in Melanesia, discussion paper, 2012/9. Canberra: The Australian National University.

McDougall, Debra. 2003. 'Fellowship and citizenship as models of national community: United Church women's fellowship in Ranongga, Solomon Islands'. *Oceania* 74(1–2): 61–80. doi. org/10.1002/j.1834-4461.2003.tb02836.x.

McLeod, Abby. 2015. 'Women's leadership in the Pacific'. *State of the Art Papers,* no. 4, Birmingham: Developmental Leadership Program (DLP).

——. 2002. 'Where are the women in Simbu politics'. *Development Bulletin* 59: 43–46.

Monson, Rebecca. 2013. 'Vernacularising political participation: Strategies of women peace-builders in Solomon Islands'. *Intersections: Gender and Sexuality in Asia and the Pacific* 33. Online: intersections. anu.edu.au/issue33/monson.htm (accessed 13 August 2016).

Nishitani, Makiko. 2014. 'Kinship, gender and communication technologies: Family dramas in the Tongan diaspora'. *The Australian Journal of Anthropology* 25(2): 207–22. doi.org/10.1111/taja.12089.

Pacific Institute of Public Policy (PiPP). 2012, *Net Effects: Social and Economic Impacts of Telecommunications and Internet in Vanuatu*. Port Vila: PiPP.

Pacific Young Women's Leadership Alliance (PYWLA). 2013. *Pacific Young Women's Leadership Alliance: Online Dialogue Issue Series.* Suva: PYWLA.

Paina, Dalcy Tovosia. 2000. 'Peacemaking in Solomon Islands: The experience of the Guadalcanal Women for Peace movement'. *Development Bulletin* 53: 47–48.

Pollard, Alice Aruhe'eta. 2003. 'Women's organizations, voluntarism, and self-financing in Solomon Islands: A participant perspective'. *Oceania* 74(1–2): 44–60.

Riles, Annelise. 2001. *The Network Inside Out.* Ann Arbor, MI: University of Michigan Press.

Spark, Ceridwen. 2014. 'Developing Young women's collective action in Vanuatu'. State Society and Governance in Melanesia, in brief, 2014/28. Canberra: The Australian National University.

——. 2010. 'Changing lives: Understanding the barriers that confront educated women in Papua New Guinea'. *Australian Feminist Studies* 25(63): 17–30. doi.org/10.1080/08164640903499901.

Spark, C. and Corbett, J. 2016. 'Archetypes, Agency and Action: Emerging Women Leaders' Views on Political Participation in Melanesia'. *International Feminist Journal of Politics.* dx.doi.org/10.1080/146167 42.2016.1189680.

Surman, Tonya and Mark Surman. 2008. *Listening to the Stars: The Constellation Model of Collaborative Social Change.* Toronto: Canadian Partnership for Children's Health and the Environment (CPCHE).

Sutton, Jo and Scarlet Pollock. 2000. 'Online activism for women's rights'. *CyberPsychology and Behaviour* 3(5): 699–706. doi.org/10.1089/10949310050191700.

Taylor, John P. 2016. 'Drinking money and pulling women: Mobile phone talk, gender, and agency in Vanuatu'. *Anthropological Forum* 26(1): 1–16. doi.org/10.1080/00664677.2015.1071238.

World YWCA. 2011. *Safe. Respect. Included. Connected. Skilled: A Pacific Young Women's Leadership Strategy (2011–2014).* Geneva: World YWCA.

7

Lewa Was Mama
(Beloved Guardian Mother)

Michelle Nayahamui Rooney
The Australian National University

Mi raun lo Sir John Guise stadium	I was at Sir John Guise stadium
Baim buai na stori tsol	Buy betel nut and chat along
Susa wokabout i kam pulim buai lo han blo mi. Mitupla lap na tok pilai	Sister approaches. From my hand she takes my betel nut. We laugh and tell a joke
Tsol em bingim han blo mi na tok lo iau blo mi	She squeeze my hand and whispers in my ear
Susa yu raun we? Lapun mama ya i painim yu	Sister where have you been? Old mother there she looks for you
Mi bekim – buai spakim mi tu	I respond – giddy with betel nut
Susa mi stap. Raun tasol. Painim wok. Mekim wok	Sister I am here. Spin around. Look for work. Make work
Kisim ol pikinini go lo skul. Yu save pinis	Take children to the school. You know the usual

Yu tok Lapun mama ya la tok wanem?	You say old mother there what talk she wants me for?
Susa em harim osem wanpla rong i painim yu	Sister she hears that something bad you came across
Mi bekim, ai raun blo buai wok lo isi nau	I respond, betel nut dizziness now easing up
Ah yu tok. Em harim se wanpla rong i kisim mi?	Ah say what – she heard something bad I came across?
Ah em harim osem. Yu stap yu traim ringim em n sekim em	Ah she heard. You should try and ring and check on her
Sekim em na painim aut wanem rong em harim	Check and find exactly what bad she heard about
Aiyo buai kik ya tanim ai blo mi na bel blo mi sut	Aye betel nut dizziness comes strong and heart it skips a beat
Wanem rong nau ya lapun mama ya i painim mi?	What wrong – what bad that old mother she look for me?
Mi raun lo Boroko, mi sekim ol kolos lo Yakaplin	I go to Boroko. I check dress at market Yakaplin
Ol kolos ya stail tumas. Sapos mi traim ating by lewa ya kalap kalap	Those stylish clothes. If I try – excited might my lover be
Lewa ya tu sa taitim masol tumas. Liklik wara na ai sa raun.	Lover too much flexing muscle. Small water and dizzy he becomes
Liklik wara na kros na jeles pasin sa pundaun. Ating mi stailim mi tumas	Small water and upon me anger and jealousy come. Maybe too much styles – me
Ol kolos tu ya nais tumas. Fifti toea, wan kina na tu kina	Oh those dresses very nice. Fifty toea, one kina and two kina
Ai sore ating mi gat fiftin kina ba mi autim displa retpla blaus	Aye if only I had fifteen kina that bright red blouse would be mine
Tasol tingting kisim masol lewa ya. Nogut em belhat nating ken	But muscle lover comes to mind. Anger he might feel again
Mi raun i go i kam. Mi tingim lapun mama ya.	I go and I come. I think of that old mother there

Maski mi traim sekim em.
Pinga paitim namba lo
mobail pon

Never mind. I try and check on
her. Fingers hit the numbers on
the mobile phone

Bip bip bip bip bip bip bip bip

Bip bip bip bip bip bip bip bip

Putim pon lo iau na harim.
Nek blo em ba kam o?

Put phone on the ear. Listen.
Will her voice come?

Putim pon lo iau

Put the phone on my ear

Halo. Halo. Yu husait? Halo.
Halo

Hello. Hello. Who are you? Hello.
Hello

Mi no harim yu. Yu wet. Ok ok
em nau

I cannot hear you. You wait.
Ok ok now is good

Yu husait ya mi tok! Yu husait
ya mi tok!

Who are you I say?! Who are
you I say?!

Maski giamanim mi mi no yangpla
meri. Yu harim? Mi lapun meri ya

Don't lie to me. I am not a pretty lass.
You hear? I am an old lady

Mi bekim. Mi bekim. Ol kolos kala
raunim ai blo mi

I respond. I respond. Dizzy from
the colourful dresses

Ol koins lo bilum pairap tu

The coins in my bilum clink as well

Halo. Lapun mama? Em mi tasol ya

Hello. Old mother? It is only me.

Susa ya em tok yu painim mi? Aiyo sori
tru mi no ringim yu

Sister said you look for me? Aye sorry
did not ring you sooner

Em yu ah? Pikinini lewa blo mi.
em yu ah?

Is that you? My beloved child.
Is that you?

Lapun mama ya em luksave lo
nek blo mi

Old mother there she heard and
recognised my voice

Ai yu em pikinini blo mi. Yu orait?

Aye! You are my child. Are you ok?

Ayee lewa pikinini blo mi long taim mi
no lukim yu

Aye my beloved child very long
time no see

Mi harim em. Ol kolos kala *ya tu ya*	I heard her. Those dress colours blinding me
Ret, yello, grin, blu, kala kala stret *na nais*	Red. Yellow. Blue. Colours. Colours – bold and nice
Spet blo buai tu ya karamapim sait	Betel spittle covering the side
Sumuk blo paia na mit em mekim *bel karai*	Fire, smoke and meat – smells make my stomach growl
Ah. Mama em mi tasol ya. Susa tok yu *painim mi?*	Ah. Mother it is only me. Sister there said you looked for me?
Yu tok. Wanpla samting yu laikim *mi mekim?*	You say. Is there something I can do?
Yu sik mama yu laik mi kukim sup *na kam?*	Are you sik mama? Shall I cook some soup?
Yu wet bai mi go maket Malaoro *painim pis na kumu mi kam kuk*	You wait let me find fish, vegies at market Malaoro. I'll come cook.
Ai lewa pikinini mi painim *yu steret*	Aye beloved child I searched for you I did
Ai taim mama tok olsem, lewa *blo mi i sut*	Aye when mama said like that my heart it skipped a beat
Wanpla rong bai em autim. Em wanem *rong steret?*	What's this wrong she will reveal? What's this bad she talks about?
Ol kolos kala sun i kukim nau. *Tingting blo mi i go lo buai ken*	Those dresses sun scorched now. Betel nut kick comes to mind
Ai lewa pikinini blo mi. nek blo mama *i wari nau*	Aye beloved child of mine. Mama's voice is worried now
Mi harim osem masol lewa ya i mekim *sampla rabis pasin*	I hear that muscle lover there he does some bad bad things
Mi harim osem em kisim wanpla *meri ken*	I hear he's has got another mistress now
Mi harim osem ai blo yu bilak yu *putim ai galas i go lo wok*	I hear that your eye is black. That you wore dark glasses into work

O tok tru yu harim
lapun mama

Ok. Old mother dear all that you
hear is true

Tasol yu save pinis em pasin maret
mipla stap

But you know these ways are
marriage ways. We are here

Em orait. Em go wok. Haste nait mipla
go raun lo tambu meri ya

It's ok. He's gone to work. Last night
we visited the sister in law

Ol pikinini orait mipla stap tasol

The children are alright. We are ok

Ai na mi kam raun ai giris long kolos lo
Yakaplin

Aye and here I am admiring clothes
at Yakaplin

Lapun mama em maret pasin tasol
– mi orait

Old mama it's just marriage ways
that is all. I'm ok

Na yu stap tasol yu no sik?

And you ok? You are not sick?

Aiyo mi stap pinis mi kam raun
painim pis

Aye I'll make sure I'll find fish
I'll come

Tasol lapun mama ya iau blong em
i no harim

But old mother there her deaf ears
did not hear

Olgeta gutpla toktok blo mi
swit tumas

All my good talk, my sweet
sweet words

Em i no harim osem mi tok
em maret pasin tasol

She did not hear me say that this
is marriage ways that's all

Het storong ya lapun mama
ya em i tok

That stubborn mother there she
continued to say

Lewa pikinini blo mi

Beloved child of mine

Wari kiliim mi turu mi
tingim yu

When I think of you I am
worried sick

Mi tingim yu bai mi halpim yu
olsem wanem?

I think of helping you. How – how
can I help?

Maret pasin em turu tasol skin blo yu
em skin blo mi

Marriage ways that's true but your
skin is my skin

Pikinini yu harim mi.	My child listen to me.
Yu harim gut	Listen very carefully
Sampla toktok blo mi yu kisim nau	My words right now you take
Yu harim mi gat sampla samting.	You listen. I have something.
Samting ya em pawa stret	This thing is powerful true
Samting ya em masol lewa bai silek.	This thing. Your beloved muscle
Yu harim? Yu klia lo tok blo mi?	will calm down. You hear?
	You understand?
Ai lapun mama yu mekim	Aye old mother what you say
bikpla tok	is very deep
Em pawa ya em wanem	What is this power thing you
samting stret?	talk about?
Na i stap we? Yu bai givim or	Where is it? Will you give it?
bai mi baim?	Will I buy?
Em lo maket or lo balus?	Is it at the market or imported?
Ai pikinini. Yu noken wari.	Aye child. Do not worry. You are
Yu em lewa blo mi stret.	my beloved child
Mi wari lo yu na mi painim	I worry for you I found this thing.
Em mi yet bai mi givim	This thing I will give to you
Noken tingting noken wari noken pret	Don't think. Don't worry.
	Don't fear.
Lapun mama na displa pawa ya	Old mother – and this power –
displa malera	this magic
Em i wel, o sop, or lip or simuk,	Is it oil, or soap, or leaves, or smoke,
o paura or wara?	or powder or water?
Em Kawar? Mi no save lukim yet	Is it ginger? I have not seen it yet.
Plis yu tok klia na mi harim	Please explain so I can hear

*Lewa pikinini em wel yu putim
lo skin blo yu*

Beloved child. It's oil you smooth
on your skin

*Lewa pikinini em ti yu tanim bai
masol lewa i diring*

Beloved child it's tea you make.
Your beloved muscle he will drink

Lewa pikini laik blo yu tasol

Beloved child it's up to you

Yu tokim mi lo laik blo yu na mi givim

Tell me if this is what you want
and I will give

Ai lapun mama. Ai lapun mama

Aye old mama. Aye old mama

*Nau em maus blo mi em pas na ai
blo mi em op*

Now my mouth is silent but my
eyes open wide

Tingting nau i go bek buai.

Betel nut comes back to mind

*Mi spetim buai ating bai tingting gut i
kisim mi*

Maybe betel nut will bring clarity
back to stay with me

Trangu lapun mama wari lo mi

Poor old mama worries about me

Trangu lapun mama tingim mi

Poor old mama she thinks of me

*Em painim wei lo halpim mi lo taim
nongut blo mi*

She finds a way to help me out when
bad times come to me

*Het blo mi i raun lo kainkain
planti tingting*

My head spins with all kinds
of thoughts

*Mi tingim laip, mi tingim
maret pasin tu ya*

I think of life, I think of marriage
ways as well

*Em sa swit na olgeta samting
em orait*

It is very sweet and everything
is alright

*Tasol taim masol lewa ya sa
apim wara*

But when beloved muscle lifts
his water

*Na han skin sa tait na han
sa slek*

And with his flexed up arms and his
hand he takes a strike

Aiyo maret pasin ya tu sa hat

Aiyo marriage ways they can be hard

Skin sa pen na maus sa buruk

Skin will hurt and mouth will break

*Lewa sa pen na kainkain wari
tingting sa kamap*

Heart aches and all kinds of worry
thoughts come up

*Aiyo maret em orait tasol masol lewa sa
tanim baksait*

Aiyo marriage is ok but beloved
muscle he can turn his back

Mama lewa yu tok ken ah	Beloved mama please say it again
Dispela samting wanem pawa stret?	This thing what power is it?
Bai mi plai lo nait? Bai mi lukim wanem?	Will I fly at night? What will I see?
Nogut masol lewa lukim mi?	Maybe muscle lover will see me?
Pikinini lewa yu sa wari nating stret	Beloved child you worry over nothing
Em i no wanpla samting nogut	It is nothing bad
Ai mi tokim yu. Em winim wel blo Kutubu. Yu rabim wel lo skin blo yu	Aye I tell you. It's better than the oil of Kutubu. You smooth this oil on your skin
Yu tanim ti na em bai dring em winim ti blo Kurumul	You boil a tea and he will drink its better than tea of Kurumul
Aiyo pikinini lewa bai olgeta wari i pinis	Aiyo beloved child all your worries will be no more
Bai masol lewa blo yu bai masol slek	Your beloved muscle his muscles will ease up
Em bai lukim yu bai lukim yangpla flawa	He will only see a young flower – that is you
Em bai lukim swit swit flawa susu i sanap	He will see a sweet sweet flower. Breasts young and tender
Aiyo pikinini lewa, masol lewa bai no nap	Aiyo beloved child muscle lover he will not
Tromoi ai i go lo narapla meri ken	Cast his eyes on another woman
Yu tasol yu bai flawa sanap stap	Only you. A flower you will stand
Wanem kainkain tingting em i gat lo narapla	All his many thoughts of another
Em bai lus tingting.	He will cast away
Masol nau sa tait lo brukim maus blo yu	Those muscles now intent on hurting you. Break your mouth
Masol ya bai slek na silip lukautim yu	Muscles will relax and lie down to care for you
Pikinini lewa olgeta wari blo yu bai ol go tu	My beloved child all your worries disappear

Yu putim wel lo skin o tanim ti em dring	You smooth this oil on skin or make tea he drinks
Tupla wantaim wankain tasol	Both are very similar
Olgeta wari blo yu bai pinis	All your worries they will disappear
Olgeta kainkain tingting em sa gat lo paul bai lus	All his thoughts of going around he will forget
Mi tokim yu em pawa stret, malera, posin,	I tell you it is powerful, Magic, Potion,
Mi tokim yu olgeta wari blo yu bai ronowei	I tell you all your worries they will run away
Mi holim stap sapos yu laik kam lukim	I hold it here in case you want to see
Mi haitim wanpla tasol stap nogut yu tok mi karim kam	I keep one only in case you want – I can bring to you
Aiyo olgeta skin blo mi kirap	Aiyo goosebumps ripple through my skin
Aiyo kainkain tingting raun lo het	Aiyo all kinds of thoughts enter my head
Ating buai nau em bai stretim displa het	I think betel nut now will straighten this here head
Lapun mama ya i tromoi toktok stret	This old mother she her talk is making sense
Ok lapun mama bai mi pinisim raun na mi kam	Ok old mother let me finish I will come
Yu stap lo we? Bai mi painim yu	Where are you? I will look for you.
Yu wetim Tunde nambaut mi bai kam	I'll come around Tuesday. You wait.
Yu harim? Displa em mi harim em i swit tumas	You hear? This thing I hear it sounds so very sweet

Mi stap mi stap na salim *planti tingting go*	I stay. I stay and dwell a lot on this
Olgeta tok blo lapun mama em orait	All her words are ok – old mother
Tasol nau lo pepa kainkain stori *sa kamap*	But now many many stories show up in the papers
Olsem malera na posin em i no *gutpla pasin*	That magic and poison are not good ways
Ol tok ol Hagen kilim *wanpla mama*	They said the Hageners killed a woman
Ol Hagen kukim mama ya lo paia	The Hageners burnt her on a fire
Olgeta man meri sanap na *lukim em*	All the men and women stood and looked at her
Ol tok pawa, malera, posin mama *ya em strong tumas*	They said her power, her magic, her poison was too strong
Poret blo ol ol kilim em ol *Hagen ya*	Their fear overcame them – those Hageners
Ol tok ol wansol Bougainville kilim *tripla meri*	They said the islanders on Bougainville three women they did kill
Ol susa ya ol mekim rong? Ol mekim *wanem rong turu?*	Did those sisters do a wrong? What wrong exactly did they do?
Na lapun mama ya em painim wei lo *halpim mi*	And old mother there she has found oil to help me out
Lapun mama ya em toktok *gut tasol*	Old mother there her words are very good
I no gat wanpla rong. Em painim *sol wei lo halpim mi*	There is nothing wrong at all. She just found way to help me out
Em wari kilim em lo mi na em i *painim mi*	She is worried sick for me and all she did is look for me
Ai planti kainkain tingting mi salim	Aye all kinds of thoughts I dwell upon

Tunde kam na Tunde go na *mi no go*	Tuesday came and Tuesday went. I did not go
Painim lapun mama ya. Mi no go	Look for old mother there. I did not go
Friday kam na masol lewa *apim wara*	Friday came and muscle lover his drink he lifted
Ai taim nogut blo mi i kam han buruk	Aye when bad times come. Broken arm

Han buruk mi go hausik go *painim marasin*	Broken arm to hospital I go. Look for medicine
Ol nes i sasim mi lo baim *han buruk*	The nurses charge me for my broken arm
Ol tok mi rong lo man *i paitim mi*	They say it's my fault – the man he fights with me
Ai masol lewa em kam lukautim *mi klostu tripla wik*	Aye nearly three weeks muscle lover there he looked after me.

Narapla Tunde kam na go. Narapla *potnait kam*	Another Tuesday comes and goes. Another fortnight comes.
Wara i kapsait olsem tais. Masol lewa *ya apim wara gut*	Water pours like a flood. Muscle lover lifts his water well
Em maret pasin tasol mi tok. *Olgeta samting i orait*	Its only marriage ways I say. Everything will be ok
Maret pasin tu ya mi tok. Taim nogut *taim wara ron mi sa kisim taim*	But marriage ways I say. When bad times come and water runs – suffering I stay

Mi tingim ol gapman nau ol tok lo *rausim pasin kilim galas meri*	I think of government now they say to get rid of sorcery killings
Mi tingim taim lapun man i sik na	I think of my old man – sick
Blut blo pisin ol glasim wok *painim aut*	The blood of a bird they used to diagnose
Husat turu em i bagarapim em. *Wanem has blo sik blem*	Who to blame for making him sick. What to blame for making him sick.

Mi tingim taim lapun man i dai na rokrok kam sindaun	I remember when my old man died and the frog came and sat
Lo dua lo haus em makim taim nogut	On the door of the house to tell us – bad news coming
Mi tingim diriman. Mi tingim sain blo tumbuna	I think of dreams I had. I think of signs of ancestors
Ai lapun mama ya em i no rong. Em wok lo wari tsol lo mi	Aye old mother there she is not wrong. She is only worried for me
Mi tingim mama karim i stori lo wanpla lapun papa blem	I think of birth mother's story of her old father in the days
Em tokim em lo bai ol i wasim em	He said to her that they must wash her too
Mama karim bekim. Ai papa yu no harim yet?	Birth mother responded. Hey old man have you not heard?
Ol lotu lain i wasim mi lo wara na Jisas em was man blo mi nau	The churchfolk washed me and Jesus he is my guardian watchman now
Na bubu man ya bekim em olsem	And Grandfather he responded like this
Pikinini em orait mi ting Jisas em i gutpla man	Child that's all right I think Jesus is a good man
Was man blo ples antap. Tasol yu save samting blong graun em i pawa tu	He will watch you from above. But as you know the spirits of the land are powerful
Olsem na bai mipla wasim yu	That is why we must anointment will protect you too
Na trangu mama karim daunim em yet nau	So poor dear birth mama. She humbled herself now
Na larim lapun papa wasim em na spetim em lo buai	She let the old man wash her. Protect her and anoint her with betel nut spittle
Kisim strong blong tumbuna na Papa Got wantem	Taking strength from ancestors and Father God as well
Em displa pasin tumbuna bin stap lo taim bipo na nau i stap lo blut	These ancestral ways have been here before and now they're in the blood

Na masol lewa ya masol i no slek

And muscle lover. Muscle did not slack

Masol lewa ya i taitim han olgeta taim

Muscle lover he always flex his arms

Na skin blo mi laik dai. Mi sa pundaun olsem lang

And my skin. It is numb. I fall down like a fly

Skin blo mi i les na wari kilim mi

My body is tired and I am worried sick.

Ol poroman blong masol lewa tu ya

And the friends of muscle lover too

Ol i tokim em olsem. Em ya kaikai kawar na spetim meri ya

To him they said like this. Here, eat this ginger and curse that woman

bai em i lusim yu. Rausim em.

She will leave you. Get rid of her,

Maus blong em i sap tumas. I gat planti resa mama stap

Her mouth is way too sharp. There are many other beauties here

Mi traim lapun mama ya mi traim em tasol

Let me try old mother there. Let me just try her and see

Pinga blo mi paitim pon

My fingers hit the phone

Bip bip bip bip bip bip bip bip

Bip bip bip bip bip bip bip bip

Lewa blo mi sut. Mi pulim win

My heart it skips a beat. I take a breath

Tasol nogat susa meri ya em tromoi inglis kam

But it's only sister on the phone in English she responds

'The person you are calling is not available. Please try again later'

'The person you are calling is not available. Please try again later'

Aiyo lapun mama ya yu go we? Yu stap o?

Aiyo old mother dear where are you? Are you there?

Em orait bai mi traim gen bihain

That's ok I will try again later

Narapla Tunde kam na go

Another Tuesday comes and goes

Bip bip bip bip bip bip bip bip

Bip bip bip bip bip bip bip bip

Susa meri tsol em bekim kam …

Only sister responds again … That's

Em orait bai mi 'try again later'

alright I will try again later

Bip bip bip bip bip bip bip bip

Bip bip bip bip bip bip bip bip

Tripla mun i lus na les lo wet mi ketsim bas i go	Three months go by and sick of waiting I catch a bus and go
Go kamap lo ples we op kat timba haus sanap. Lapun mama. Yu stap?	I arrive at the place where the off cut timber house stands. Mama are you there?
Trangu taim mi go kamap i nogat haus i stap. Sit blo paia tsol i bilasim graun	Alas when I arrive there is no house but ashes decorate the ground
Aweee mi sakim het. Na op kat haus? I bin sanap lo hia	Aweee I shake my head. Off cut house? It used to stand right here
Isi tasol mi askim ol lain lo sait sait haus	Whispering I asked the neighbours nearby
Ay plis yupla lukim lapun mama ya? Em go raun?	Aye please have you seen this old mama here? Has she gone out?
Ssss weeesshh susa meri yu husat? Yu lewa pikinini?	Shhh weeeeshh sister girl who are you? Are you beloved child?
Sori tru lapun mama go pinis	Sorry true but old mother she has gone
Mipla kisim kainkain tingting na bel hevi	We were faced with all sorts of thoughts and worries too
Lapun mama ya em pawa meri stret na bilum i pulap	That old mother she was very powerful. Her bag was full of stuff
Malera, kambang, posin, kawar glass meri em em stret	Magic. Lime. Poison. Ginger. Sorceress she was that is true
Olgeta pawa ya em holim stap na pawa blem i winim mipela	All the powers that she had they overcame us you see
Poret em kisim mipla taim harim kainkain masalai	We were filled with fear when we heard all sorts of spirits
Na pisin krai lo nait. Ol meri Samarai palai lo bik moning	And birds they call at night. Samarai women they fly over near dawn
Rokrok singaut na binatang i dai lo winduo	Frogs they call and bees drop dead on the window sill
Mipla kisim taim lo kainkain birua tingting	We were faced with all sorts of thoughts and worries too

Olsem na ol man i makim maus blo mipla ol it tok

So the men who represent.
The men they said

Ol i tok. Em mas go! Em i mas go na ples bai orait ken!

They said. She must go! She must go and our place will be safe again!

Susa lewa mipla kukim haus blo em olsem na sit blo paia yu lukim

Beloved sister so we burnt her house.
That's the ashes that you see.

Trangu kilim em nogat tasol ronim em mipla sutim ston

Poor thing. Kill her we did not.
But chase her we did and we did so throwing stones

Ayee nau em bikpla wari tingting kisim mi

Ayee I am overcome now with concern for her

Em go we? Mi askim ol. Em orait? Mi askim ol

Where did she go? I ask of them.
Is she ok? I asked of them

Em mama lewa blo mi stret na yupla ronim em

She is my beloved mother how could you chase her so

Wai na tripla mun i lus mi wet na painim pis?

Why did I wait three months? Find fish and come to her.

Ol gutpla lain ol tokim mi

Some good folks they told me this

Susa noken pret lapun mama mipla harim

Sister have no fear. Old mother there we have heard

Lapun mama go painim pemili lo Morata

Old mother has gone to family at Morata

Em no dai tasol hia em noken kam bek no gut bel hat pasin i kamap

She did not die but here she must not return. In case angry ways arise

Ayee gutpla tingting i kisim mi

Ayee now my thoughts are calmer now

Em i no dai. Em i ronowei go Morata

She did not die. She has runaway to Morata

Em orait bip bip bip bip bip bip bip bip

That's ok. Bip bip bip bip bip bip bip bip

Susa meri tasol bekim Inglis kam … 'try again later'

Sister lady only English she responds … 'try again later'

177

Tunde kam na Tunde go narapla tripla mun i lus	Tuesday comes and Tuesday goes. Another three more months pass by
Bip bip bip bip bip bip bip bip	Bip bip bip bip bip bip bip bip
Aiyo mama lewa mi salim tingting kam	Aiyo beloved mother my thoughts I send to you
Wai na mi no harim tok blo yu	Why did I not heed your counsel
Maret pasin em tasol i no wanpla samting tu	It's only marriage ways. It's really no big deal
Maret pasin em tasol. Masol lewa apim wara	Only marriage ways. Muscle lover takes his drink
Masol lewa paitim mi, skin i pen, blut i kapsait	Muscle lover beats me up. Body hurts. Blood – it pours down
Masol lewa kisim narapla, na narapla na narapla meri ken	Muscle lover takes another and another and another woman again
Ating sapos mi harim yu – was mama lewa, lapun mama	Perhaps if I had taken heed – guardian beloved mother. Old mother
Ating sapos mi harim yu masol lewa ya bai dai lo mi tasol	Perhaps if I had taken heed. Muscle lover – in love with me alone
Ating bai maret pasin stap orait	Maybe marriage life would be alright
Ating bai pemili tu bai sindaun gut	Maybe family life would be ok
Em orait na nau mi salim tingting tsol	That's ok. So now I think of you and ponder these
Mi bai bip bip bip bip bip bip bip bip	I will bip bip bip bip bip bip bip bip
Inap swit nek blo yu pairap lo pon lewa was mama blo mi	Until I hear your sweet voice on the phone. My beloved guardian mother
Diriman na wetim wanpla gutpla taim bai masol lewa ya i dai lo mi tasol.	Dream and stay and wait for one fine day when muscle lover would die for me alone.

Afterword for *Lewa Was Mama*

Lewa Was Mama—Beloved Guardian Mother—can be considered an ethnographic poem (Denzin 1997; Maynard and Cahnmann-Taylor 2010). It is reflexive auto-ethnography (Ellis, Adams and Bochner 2011; Reed-Danahay 2001) and in this afterword I elaborate its context and relation to the themes of this collection. The poem is set in Port Moresby, the capital city of Papua New Guinea (PNG), where I was born and lived for many years. It draws on decades of life stories and experiences, including those from fieldwork for my PhD, which was conducted over a six-month period from January to June 2013. I wrote the poem—or perhaps more truthfully, the poem came to me—after returning from my fieldwork. As I started to sift through my data, I found myself struggling to reconcile gaps between the big picture development narratives about women's empowerment and the intimate details of the day-to-day lives of the many women I knew.

The starting place for the poem is the Sir John Guise Stadium, a key feature of the city's landscape and the site of many national celebrations, such as Independence Day, sports and an important national campaign calling for action on violence against women. For many years it also played a part in my family's daily routine. Watching soccer training and games, walking around the stadium for exercise, and catching up with family or friends meant hanging around the informal markets in and around the stadium.

The poem's narrator, a woman who resides in the city, leads the reader from the stadium on some of her typical outings around the city as she reasons through her own dilemmas in love and marriage (similar to those discussed by Ceridwen Spark and Jenny Munro in this volume). She must contend with the dilemma she faces when offered help to deal with her marital problems by her elderly friend—*Lewa Was Mama*—who lives in a Moresby settlement. Boroko is a residential suburb. Morata is a suburb into which merges one of the city's larger and older informal settlements. Malaoro is one of the larger fresh food markets and Yakaplin is one of the largest used clothing markets in the city. Kutubu is the site of one of PNG's oil projects located in the highlands region at Lake Kutubu. Kurumul tea comes from the Kurumul tea plantation, also located in the highlands region of PNG.

The poem is set in 2013 when PNG and various international agencies were grappling to understand and find solutions to the epidemic of violence in PNG, which includes sorcery and domestic violence.

Sorcery and gendered violence: A humanitarian crisis

Just months before I commenced my fieldwork in 2013, the non-government organisation (NGO) Doctors Without Borders (Médecins Sans Frontières, MSF) declared the prevalence of sexual and domestic gendered violence in PNG to be a humanitarian crisis. Sadly, 2013 turned out to be a significant year for the narrative of violence in PNG's history. In February, shockwaves were felt through the international community as news and graphic images emerged of Kepari Leniata, a 20-year-old woman in Mt Hagen. Leniata had been set alight after she was accused of sorcery and burnt to death in broad daylight in front of hundreds of onlookers. In April, the world learned that in Bougainville four women had been abducted after being accused of practising sorcery. One—Helen Rumbali—was beheaded and the other three held captive for several weeks. A foreign national was gang raped in Madang around this time.

National responses

In many ways, these events led to an awakening in PNG of the need to address violence. As part of this, a movement to hold a national *Haus Krai* to acknowledge the crisis of gendered violence in PNG emerged. *Haus Krai* is the Tok Pisin term for a house or site of mourning, where people gather to mourn a deceased person. As the movement gained momentum, a number of *Haus Krai* events were held throughout the world to express solidarity with the victims of violence and to call for action to address violence in PNG.

In Port Moresby the national *Haus Krai* was held at the Sir John Guise stadium. I was conducting fieldwork while following these events and in May 2013, attended the national *Haus Krai* in the city.

The space between national and international responses and lived experiences

After fieldwork my evenings would involve catching up on personal and mainstream news via Facebook. As there was no television where we were living, Facebook was an important way for me to keep abreast of the *Haus Krai* movement. Despite being a 15-minute drive from the Sir John Guise stadium where people were gathered, I noticed a difference between the lived reality of my life and that of the people with whom I was interacting in the field. Many people in the settlement community had phones but because of a lack of electricity they generally were off because the batteries were flat or to preserve them for the most important calls. People asked if I had brought newspapers with me as a way to catch up on the news, but also to add to their stocks of toilet paper used in the pit toilets. A few houses had TVs and there were a few communal TVs, but most people seemed unaware of the national *Haus Krai* movement.

Yet violence was intimately interwoven in the day-to-day stories of struggle and survival (see Jolly 2012; Jolly, Stewart with Brewer (eds) 2012): a woman slashed with a knife by her brother-in-law; a woman beaten; a family chased from their home because one of its members was accused of sorcery; stories of love and magic to help allay a man's violent tendencies or tame his indiscretions; women elders caring for their grandchildren in the absence of parents; an elderly grandmother caring for her orphaned grandchildren after their parents had died of AIDS; and community leaders striving to address development needs while battling in courts to stay forceful evictions.

Celebrating indigenous spirituality: Sisterhood and motherhood

In my life, a dream or the sighting of a specific animal or other 'sign' conveys a meaning and is usually reflected upon to anticipate the future or explain the past. Traditional legends of women, love, seduction, magic, sorcery, weaving, gardening and life also resonate in my memory. The lived realities of many women I know reflect this same rich interweaving of the spiritual and the worldly. This poem is a celebration of the indigenous spirituality—as opposed to indigenous sorcery and witchcraft.

The space between the public responses to violence that highlight the brutality and the private narratives of witchcraft and magic relates to the more positive and spiritual magical effects that are also elements of the supernatural. As I watched the news of Leniata and Rumbali in disbelief, my emotional response involved my understandings of positive stories of spirituality. Were these phenomena one and the same thing? How had their communities judged these women so harshly when these communities placed value on their embodiment of spiritual good? By believing in my own version of spirituality was I complicit in 'practice' that so terrified communities?

Martha Macintyre noted in her work among Tubetube people that 'stories about witches and spirit beings of various sorts provide far richer material on Tubetube ideas of embodiment, social and individual morality, and personhood' that 'constitute a discourse on embodiment' (Macintyre 1995: 40). *Lewa Was Mama* may well be viewed as such a discourse about the embodiment of contemporary Melanesian femininity. *Lewa Was Mama* is the 'pivotal antinomy' (ibid.: 42). To her community, she embodies the anti-social female witch; to her young friend she offers spiritual protection, love and healing. As for the people of Tubetube (Macintyre 1995), the stories of *Lewa Was Mama* and her friend are interwoven with conflict and violence.

In this space between the public responses to violence and the private lives of those experiencing it lies the less discussed narrative—that of the mutual support women give each other. The poem celebrates the 'mutuality of being' (Sahlins 2014: 62) in which women are mutually constituted (ibid.) through sisterhood and motherhood. In the way the Melanesian person is relational and partible (Strathern 1988), so too the Melanesian woman in relation to herself and other women can be regarded as relational and partible. This feminine connection and support as well as the full extent of the impact of violence is often rendered invisible when women are cast as individual victims, rather than socially connected. The poem is both a celebration of bonds between women and of indigenous spirituality—in its many unfathomable forms. Reflecting back to when I wrote the poem, I privileged the feminine voice and feminine relationality even though I often criticise Western feminist discourses for not being culturally sensitive to PNG women's lived experiences, anchored in social relationships that include men. The poem explores the relationships and exchanges that women conduct among themselves in ways that 'acknowledge male domination and gender violence [and in doing so, they make possible] radical changes in gender relations, even perhaps in the models of the person' (Jolly 2012: 5; also see Macintyre 1995 for a discussion). By contrast, but similarly highlighting the ruptures in gender relations that contemporary life has produced, Stephanie Lusby's chapter (this volume) enables us to see our own complicity in perpetuating gendered violence when we ignore the intersection between producing security and male aggression.

I hope that by foregrounding feminine narratives of women's relationality and opposing the violence they experience, *Lewa Was Mama* enables us to see how narratives of 'women's empowerment' potentially can work to diminish the relationships that women draw on for mutual support. They can also background the broader impacts of violence on communities or networks of women who suffer collectively. The national *Haus Krai* movement is a public performance of this collective suffering but still speaks to the masculine state domain, to intervene and address violence perpetrated by men on women. *Lewa Was Mama* and her younger friend feel each other's pain as women and try to support each other through friendship and material (fish) and spiritual (magic) gifts.

In another example of changing gendered landscapes, Tait Brimacombe (this volume) discusses how the advent of mobile phones and social media platforms are providing women with avenues to participate in dialogue that would not previously have been possible. Similarly, indigenous spiritual connections also are being revolutionised by technology. In *Lewa Was Mama*, the two women never actually meet in person but this does not lessen the intensity of the feelings and emotional interactions between them. After the initial message conveyed at the market by their mutual friend—a sister—they communicate primarily through their mobile phones, or through the community from which *Lewa Was Mama* has fled. Mobile phones facilitate conversations about such issues.

Transformation and intergenerational mutuality

Lewa Was Mama shows how mutual constitution of women is also intergenerational. In embodying this spirituality, older women especially find ways of passing their knowledge on to younger generations. This shapes gender and transformation in the Pacific.

When I ask my birth mother about her early years in the 1940s, she describes them simply. She was born in a small hamlet called N'Drayongai in the Lahan area of Bulihan village on Manus Island. At birth she was wrapped in traditional bark cloth, *n'drih*. As a girl she slept in a hessian bag that had been used for copra. Her mother suffered from leprosy and was sent to far off New Ireland for treatment. She never saw her mother again. When the news reached her family that her mother had died, succumbed to her leprosy, her father decided to withdraw her from the new colonial school so she could care for her two younger sisters. Enthusiastic to attend school, she went on a hunger strike for several days until he relented. Frustrated and angry, her father allowed her to return to school—'Go to school and see where it will get you!'—he scolded her. As a young woman, while away from her home, she converted to Christianity but could not resist her elders' insistence that she be 'washed' to 'protect' her from earthly spiritual forces. As a mother, she and others acknowledge the presence of loved ones passed, who gently lit up the evenings with their flickering glow— the fireflies—ensuring our *lukaut* (care). Her stories and those of others told to us as children, transfer their indigenous personhoods and inform our understandings and our own enactment of this spirituality even in the urban context. She—Nahau Kambuou Rooney—while helping to care for her younger sisters and remaining anchored in the family that raised her, went on to become PNG's second ever female-elected Member of Parliament in 1977 and PNG's first female cabinet minister.

The personal stories of women's cultural and social roots, including their adaptive strategies and challenges, can become obscured in the overarching development narratives around women's empowerment. Dame Carol Kidu, Julie Soso, Enny Moaitz, Dame Josephine Abaijah, Margaret Nakikus, Felecia Dobunaba, Rose Kekedo, Naomi Martin, Meg Taylor, Anne Dickson-Waiko, Orovu Sepoe, Waliyato Clowes, Nahau Kambuou Rooney and others all rose to the top in their fields (Macintyre, this volume) while navigating their own PNG sociality with the professional and international demands placed on them. Women's status in Melanesia reflects their ability to adapt to place-determined socioeconomic and political factors that shape how women are seen, factors that usually place the traditional in opposition to the modern (Soaki, this volume). These oppositions privilege men and are often amplified in the urban context (for a discussion see Soaki, this volume; Spark, this volume; Cox, this volume).

Lewa Was Mama seeks to foreground the complexity of this spiritual and social connection between women in PNG and how it possibly plays an important part in enabling them to adapt and navigate the complex and sometimes inexplicable terrain of tradition, modernity, love, nurture, hope, joy, pain, violence and conflict. When the cameras have been turned off, the development workshops have ended and the national and international movements lose their momentum, this connection also enables them to retain a sense of self. It enables them to retain a degree of distance from universalising gender equality discourses that seem to prefer to ascribe 'success-hood' or 'victim-hood' to the singular woman. As Macintyre (this volume) states, 'Melanesian social worlds are in flux'. I hope that *Lewa Was Mama* makes visible some of the contributing factors and adaptive responses to this state of flux.

References

Denzin, Norman K. 1997. *Interpretive Ethnography: Ethnographic Practices for the 21st Century.* Thousand Oaks, London and New Delhi: Sage Publications. doi.org/10.4135/9781452243672.

Ellis, Carolyn, Tony E. Adams and Arthur P. Bochner. 2011. 'Autoethnography: An overview'. *Historical Social Research* 36: 273–90.

Jolly, Margaret. 2012. 'Introduction—Engendering violence in Papua New Guinea: Persons, power and perilous transformations'. In *Engendering Violence in Papua New Guinea*, ed. Margaret Jolly, Christine Stewart with Carolyn Brewer, pp. 1–46. Canberra: ANU E Press. Online: press.anu.edu.au/publications/engendering-violence-papua-new-guinea (accessed 12 August 2016).

Jolly, Margaret, Christine Stewart with Carolyn Brewer (eds). 2012. *Engendering Violence in Papua New Guinea.* Canberra: ANU E Press. Online: press.anu.edu.au/publications/engendering-violence-papua-new-guinea (accessed 12 August 2016).

Macintyre, Martha. 1995. 'Violent bodies and vicious exchanges: Personification and objectification in the Massim'. *Social Analysis: The International Journal of Social and Cultural Practice* 37 (April): 29–43.

Maynard, Kent and Melisa Cahnmann-Taylor. 2010. 'Anthropology at the edge of words: Where poetry and ethnography meet'. *Anthropology and Humanism* 35(1): 2–19. doi.org/10.1111/j.1548-1409.2010.01049.x.

Reed-Danahay, Deborah. 2001. 'Autobiography, intimacy and ethnography'. In *Handbook of Ethnography*, ed. Paul Atkinson, Amanda Coffey, Sara Delamont, John Lofland and Lyn Lofland, pp. 407–11. London, Thousand Oaks, New Delhi: Sage Publications. doi.org/10.4135/9781848608337.n28.

Sahlins, M. 2014. *What Kinship Is – And Is Not*. Chicago and London: University of Chicago Press.

Strathern, Marilyn. 1988. *The Gender of the Gift: Problems with Women and Problems with Society in Melanesia*. Berkeley and Los Angeles, CA: University of California Press. doi.org/10.1525/california/9780520064232.001.0001.

Contributors

Tait Brimacombe holds Bachelor's degrees in Development Studies and Law from the University of Adelaide, and began her PhD in 2012 in the Department of Anthropology and Development Studies at the University of Adelaide investigating the intersection of communication for development and gender in the Pacific. Tait has also contributed to research for AusAID (now the Department of Foreign Affairs and Trade) and the Australian Civil Military Centre on communication for development in fragile states, and the role of communication in complex emergencies. Tait is currently a Developmental Leadership Program Research Fellow in the Institute for Human Security and Social Change, La Trobe University. Her current research interests include women's leadership, coalitions and collective action in the Pacific.

John Cox is an Honorary Lecturer at the School of Culture, History and Languages, The Australian National University. He has 20 years' experience in the Pacific as a volunteer, program manager, consultant and anthropologist. His PhD research on fast money schemes in Papua New Guinea was awarded the Australian Anthropological Society Prize for Best PhD Thesis 2012. He has published several articles on this topic and is finalising a monograph that will be published by Indiana University Press.

Stephanie Lusby is a PhD candidate with the State, Society and Governance in Melanesia Program at The Australian National University. Her recent research focuses on how men in Papua New Guinea respond to campaigns aimed at transforming gender norms in order to prevent HIV and violence against women. She is particularly interested in how campaign messages have been incorporated into ideas of aspirational masculinity, and how men's reading of those messages is shaped by their attempts to navigate economic, environmental and political uncertainty. Stephanie is also the Program Manager (Pacific) at International Women's

Development Agency. In this role she facilitates partnerships with women's rights organisations focused on improving women's access to civic and political participation.

Martha Macintyre is currently a Principal Research Fellow in Anthropology in the School of Social Sciences at the University of Melbourne. She was editor of the Australian Anthropological Society's flagship journal, *TAJA*, from 2008–2015. In 2012 she was elected a Fellow of the Academy of Social Sciences in Australia. Her early anthropological research focused on the economic and social effects of colonial intrusion in Tubetube, Milne Bay Province. More recently, she has concentrated on gender inequality and the broad social changes associated with resource extractive industries in Melanesia. She has published extensively on human rights and the status of women. Her publications include *Human Rights and Gender Politics: Perspectives on the Asia Pacific Region*, edited with Anne-Marie Hildson, Vera Mackie, and Maila Stivens (Abington: Routledge, 2000); *Managing Modernity in the Western Pacific*, edited with Mary Patterson (St Lucia: University of Queensland Press, 2011); and *Gender Violence & Human Rights: Seeking Justice in Fiji, Papua New Guinea & Vanuatu*, edited with Aletta Biersack and Margaret Jolly (Canberra: ANU Press, 2015).

Jenny Munro is a cultural anthropologist who has worked in Papua/West Papua since 2006. She is co-editor (with Martin Slama) of *From 'Stone Age' to 'Real Time': Exploring Papuan Temporalities, Mobilities and Religiosities* (Canberra: ANU Press, 2015). Jenny's other publications explore education, racism, HIV/AIDS, alcohol, and pregnancy in Papua/West Papua. Jenny is a research fellow in the Coral Bell School of Asia Pacific Affairs at The Australian National University, where she also co-convenes the annual Pacific Research Colloquium and teaches in the Master of Applied Anthropology and Participatory Development.

Michelle Nayahamui Rooney is a Research Fellow at the Development Policy Centre, The Australian National University. Michelle holds a Master of Arts in Development Economics from University of Sussex, UK, and a Bachelor of Economics (Honours) from ANU. Her research is interdisciplinary and engages with economic anthropology, human geography and political economy to examine urban life in PNG and its intersection with migration, gender, economic engagement, inequality social safety nets, security, and land and housing.

Pauline Soaki is a Solomon Islander who is currently Director for Women's Development Division in the Ministry of Women, Youth, Children and Family Affairs in Solomon Islands. After completing a BA in Sociology and Politics at the University of the South Pacific in Fiji, she gained a Master's in Development Studies, specialising in Gender and Development from the University of Melbourne, Australia. Her thesis was on women's political participation in Solomon Islands. Pauline has eight years community development experience, working in the donor sector prior to taking up her position with government. She was a board member of the YWCA in 2010–2011, and is currently a board member for Women's Rights Action Movement (WRAM) and *Seif Ples,* a gender-based violence crisis and referral clinic in Honiara.

Ceridwen Spark is Vice Chancellor's Senior Research Fellow in the Centre for Global Research in the School of Global, Urban and Social Studies at RMIT University in Melbourne. Ceridwen writes about gender and social change in Papua New Guinea and the Pacific. More recently, she has focused on the relationship between gender and spatiality in the region's rapidly developing urban centres. Ceridwen has published extensively, including in anthropology, feminist studies and sociology journals. She enjoys working with diverse people and methods to produce films, digital stories and exhibitions that reach audiences beyond the academy.

www.ingramcontent.com/pod-product-compliance
Lightning Source LLC
Chambersburg PA
CBHW040153270326
41928CB00040B/3329